ASVAB STUDY GUIDE
READING SKILLS

Reading Skill Preparation & Strategies and Paragraph Comprehension Practice Tests for the ASVAB Test and AFQT

The ASVAB and AFQT are registered trademarks of the United States Department of Defense, which is not affiliated with nor endorses this publication.

ASVAB Study Guide Reading Skills: Reading Skill Preparation & Strategies and Paragraph Comprehension Practice Tests for the ASVAB Test and AFQT

© COPYRIGHT 2016

Exam SAM Study Aids & Media dba www.examsam.com

All rights reserved. No part of this publication may be reproduced, stored in a retrieval system, or transmitted, in any form or by any means, electronic, mechanical, photocopying, recording, or otherwise, without the prior written permission of the copyright owner.

ISBN-13: 978-1-949282-11-5

ISBN-10: 1-949282-11-2

For information on bulk discounts, please contact us at: email@examsam.com

NOTE: The ASVAB and AFQT are registered trademarks of the United States Department of Defense, which is not affiliated with nor endorses this publication.

ASVAB AND AFQT TEST INFORMATION

The ASVAB Examination (Armed Services Vocational Aptitude Battery) assesses your skills for a career in the military.

The ASVAB is administered both on the computer and in traditional pencil and paper format. The complete pencil-and-paper ASVAB consists of eight sections, while the complete computer-assisted ASVAB consists of nine sections.

You should enquire at your testing location to see which version of the exam they are offering.

If you are still in high school, you should ask your guidance counselor if the ASVAB exam is going to be offered at your school.

You can also take the ASVAB at a Military Entrance Processing Station (MEPS) or at a Mobile Examination Team Site (METS.)

Your guidance counselor or testing officer can also provide information about how you will receive your score report.

You can retake the ASVAB if you are not satisfied with your score. However, there are restrictions associated with retaking the exam, so it will be to your benefit to be well-prepared for your exam when you first take it.

Your AFQT score for the examination consists of only four of the sections of the ASVAB: Word Knowledge, Paragraph Comprehension, Arithmetic Reasoning, and Mathematics Knowledge.

The AFQT (Armed Forces Qualifying Test) score is the most important score for entrance into the military, and you will need to have a certain AFQT score in order to be eligible to enlist. Your AFQT score is also used to decide what kinds of jobs you will be eligible for in the armed services.

Since your AFQT score is so important, you may want to devote extra attention to studying for the AFQT sections of the exam.

INFORMATION FOR EDUCATORS

If you are an educator, please respect copyright law. This book cannot be photocopied or reproduced electronically for use with students.

In order to use the book in a classroom or tutorial setting, you should purchase a copy of the book for each of your students.

For those interested in purchasing sets of materials for classroom use, please contact us for information on bulk discounts. We may be contacted by filling in the "Contact Us" form at www.examsam.com.

HOW TO USE THIS PUBLICATION

The paragraph comprehension practice tests in this study guide contain questions of all of the types that you will see on the real ASVAB test.

Practice test 1 in this book is in "tutorial mode."

As you complete practice test 1, you should pay special attention to the tips highlighted in the special boxes.

Although you will not see tips like this on the actual exam, these suggestions will help you improve your performance on each subsequent practice test in this publication.

You should also study the explanations to the answers to practice test 1 especially carefully.

Studying the tips and explanations in reading practice test 1 will help you obtain strategies to improve your performance on the other practice tests in this book, as well as on your actual ASVAB test.

In order to simulate exam conditions, you should allow thirteen minutes to take each practice test.

FURTHER ASVAB PRACTICE

In order to do your best on the day of your test, you may also like to consider our other publications:

ASVAB Word Knowledge Workbook: Review of ASVAB Vocabulary and Word Knowledge Practice Tests for the ASVAB Test and AFQT

ASVAB Arithmetic Reasoning Practice Tests: ASVAB Arithmetic Study Guide and Arithmetic Reasoning Practice Tests for the ASVAB Test and AFQT

ASVAB Practice Test Book - Mathematics Knowledge: ASVAB Math Study Guide and Mathematics Knowledge Practice Tests for the ASVAB Test and AFQT

TABLE OF CONTENTS

Format of the ASVAB Paragraph Comprehension Test	1
Strategies and Tips for the ASVAB Paragraph Comprehension Test	2
ASVAB Paragraph Comprehension – Practice Test 1 with Answers	
Main idea questions	7
Specific detail questions	9
Determining the author's purpose, tone, or attitude	11
Understanding steps in a process	14
Making inferences and drawing conclusions	16
Understanding words in the context of the passage	17
ASVAB Paragraph Comprehension – Practice Test 2	22
Answers and Explanations – Practice Test 2	33
ASVAB Paragraph Comprehension – Practice Test 3	37
Answers and Explanations – Practice Test 3	47
ASVAB Paragraph Comprehension – Practice Test 4	50
Answers and Explanations – Practice Test 4	59
ASVAB Paragraph Comprehension – Practice Test 5	63
Answers and Explanations – Practice Test 5	77
ASVAB Paragraph Comprehension – Practice Test 6	81
Answers and Explanations – Practice Test 6	91

ASVAB Paragraph Comprehension – Practice Test 7	94
Answers and Explanations – Practice Test 7	105
ASVAB Paragraph Comprehension – Practice Test 8	109
Answers and Explanations – Practice Test 8	120

Format of the ASVAB Paragraph Comprehension Test

The ASVAB Paragraph Comprehension Test contains fifteen questions.

You may see long or short passages on this part of the ASVAB AFQT.

You will be allowed only 13 minutes to complete the Paragraph Comprehension Test, so you will need tips and strategies in order to work quickly and to help manage the time.

The biggest piece of advice that you need for the Paragraph Comprehension Test is as follows:

- **Be sure to read the questions for each passage BEFORE reading the passage itself.**
- **This will help you anticipate what to look for as you read the paragraphs.**

Bearing the above advice in mind, you should now go to the next section for specific strategies for each type of question that you may encounter on the ASVAB Paragraph Comprehension Test.

Strategies and Tips for the ASVAB Paragraph Comprehension Test

There are ten types of questions on the paragraph comprehension subtest of the ASVAB.

Paragraph comprehension questions may be placed into the following categories:

Questions asking you to identify the main idea of the passage

Main idea questions may be of three types:

1) The question may simply ask: What is the main idea?

2) The question may ask: What is the best title for this passage?

3) The passage may show numbered sentences. You then have to select which sentence from the passage best states its main idea.

TIPS FOR MAIN IDEA QUESTIONS

- For these types of questions, you have to ignore answer choices that give specific points mentioned in the passage.

- For main idea questions, you have to determine the primary purpose or overall point of the passage.

- To answer these types of questions correctly, you should identify the thesis statement of the reading passage.

- Remember that the thesis statement explains the main point of the passage.

- The thesis statement is normally included in the first paragraph of the passage, and it is very often the first or last sentence of the first paragraph.

- The incorrect answer choices will contain some specific details from the passage, but for this type of question think generally, instead of getting distracted by specific points.

Questions asking you about some specific detail in the passage

Specific detail questions may be of two types:

4) The question may ask you for information that supports or does not support a specific detail from the passage.

5) The question may ask you to identify the sequence of steps in a process that is described in the passage.

TIPS FOR SPECIFIC DETAIL QUESTIONS

- For these types of questions, you have to ignore answer choices that are too general.

- Therefore, be sure you choose a specific answer.

- In other words, you should ignore answer choices that cover the main idea of the passage or that give general information.

- Specific detail paragraph comprehension questions sometimes begin with the phrases "according to the passage" or "the passage states that."

- Questions in this category rely on your ability to search through the passage and find a specific piece of information.

- The distractor answers will be of three types:

    a) specific information that does not answer the question

    b) information that is too general

    c) answers that seem correct but which are not directly stated in the text

Questions asking you to interpret information from the passage

Interpretation questions may be of two types:

6) The question may ask you what the passage implies or what can be inferred from the passage.

7) The question may ask you to make an assumption or to draw a conclusion.

TIPS FOR INTERPRETATION QUESTIONS

- "Imply" means to suggest something without stating it directly.

- Inference or interpretation questions ask you to read between the lines of the passage and draw conclusions.

- Inference or implication questions sometimes begin with the phrases "the passage implies" or "it can be inferred from the passage that."

- The word "suggests" is sometimes substituted for "implies."

- Remember that these questions are asking you to make only a very small logical conclusion based upon information that is clearly stated in the passage.

- So, you will need to find the specific sentence in the passage that provides the basis for the conclusion given in the correct answer choice.

- Incorrect answer choices will require significant assumptions or "wild guesses."

Vocabulary in context questions

Vocabulary questions are of one general type:

8) The question will ask you to interpret the meaning of a word or phrase from the passage.

TIPS FOR VOCABULARY QUESTIONS

- Very carefully re-read the sentence that contains the word or phrase in the question.

- Look for synonyms in the passage that may be similar in meaning to the unknown word or phrase.

Application questions that ask you to determine the author's purpose

Application questions may be of two general types:

9) The question may ask you to determine the purpose of the author or of the passage.

10) The question may ask you about the author's tone, attitude, opinions, or assumptions.

TIPS FOR QUESTIONS ON THE AUTHOR

- For these types of questions, you first need to consider the tone and style of the passage.

- To determine the tone, look for opinion words in the passage such as "best" or "most important."

- Then make a logical conclusion about the author's opinion or purpose based on the tone and style.

ASVAB Paragraph Comprehension – Practice Test 1

Question 1 refers to the following passage.

A true feat of modern engineering, the Alaska Highway was constructed to link Edmonton in Alberta, Canada, to Fairbanks, Alaska. The first step in completing the mammoth project was to plan the exact route that the road was going to take. Ground and aerial surveys were conducted only slightly in advance of the construction of the road, with the survey teams working just miles ahead of the construction crew in some cases. Apart from the challenges inherent in building a road in such inclement conditions, bridges had to be erected and culverts had to be laid in drainage ditches. Swampland along the route was a further complication, and efforts to avoid the waterlogged ground created many bends in the road.

1. The main idea of this passage is that:

    A. The construction of the Alaska Highway was hampered by inclement weather.

    B. Many difficulties surrounded the planning of the Alaska Highway.

    C. The construction of the Alaska Highway was an indisputably impressive achievement.

    D. The construction of major highways usually involves ground and road surveys.

This is an example of a question on the main idea of a passage. These types of questions are very common on the Paragraph Comprehension subtest. For main idea questions, pay special attention to the first and last sentences of the passage. Also look for descriptive words in the passage, such as "problems" or "difficulties." Remember that questions on the main idea may also ask you for the best title.

Tips and Explanations:

1. The correct answer is C.

   The passage is stating that the construction of the Alaska Highway was an indisputably impressive achievement. We know this because of the word "feat" in the first sentence, as well as the words "inherent challenges" and "complication" later in the passage. You may be tempted to choose answer B, but the passage focuses on the construction of the road, not the planning. Answers A and D are incorrect because they are too general.

Question 2 refers to the following passage.

Gibberellins are a complex group of plant hormones that are involved in many botanical processes. Commonly used in combination with similar botanical hormones called auxins, their primary function is to promote plant growth by controlling the elongation of cells. They also promote the formation of fruit and seed, as well as delay aging in leaves. Having become important for commercial reasons in recent years, the hormones are also used to help meet the ever-growing demand for new hybrids of plants and flowers.

2. Which of the following best describes the botanical significance of gibberellins?

    A. Without them, plant hormones would be involved in more processes.

    B. Because of gibberellins, plants cells enlarge, thereby causing plants to grow.

    C. Leaves age more quickly, owing to the function of gibberellins.

    D. Gibberellins have nocuous consequences for fruits and seeds.

> This is an example of a question asking you for specific details from a passage. "Specific detail" questions are also very common on the ASVAB exam. For these types of questions, you need to look at each answer choice and then scan the passage to see if that fact is stated in the passage.

Tips and Explanations:

2. The correct answer is B. Gibberellins are of botanical significance because they cause plants cells to enlarge, thereby causing plants to grow. The passage states that the primary function of gibberellins "is to promote plant growth by controlling the elongation of cells." The other answer choices are not supported by the passage.

Question 3 refers to the following passage.

According to Stephen Krashen's input hypothesis, a language learner improves his or her language skills when he or she is exposed to language input such as lectures or reading materials that are one level above the learner's current level of language ability. The learner's language output, such as verbal or written expressions, is not seen to have any direct correlation to his or her actual learning ability.

3. Which of the following statements is NOT supported by the passage?

   A. Spoken language does not reflect the learner's real skills.

   B. Learners can best improve their language skills when their learning is appropriately challenging.

   C. Traditional grammatical skills are of no importance for language learning.

   D. Stephen Krashen has developed a theory on language learning.

> This is a different type of "specific detail" question. For these types of questions, you will be asked which of the answers is NOT supported by the passage. Like the previous type of question, you need to compare each of the answer choices to the specific details stated in the passage.

Tips and Explanations:

3. The correct answer is C.

    Answer A is supported by the last sentence of the passage. Answer B is supported by the statement that lectures or reading materials should be "one level above the learner's current level of language ability." Answer D is supported by the introductory phrase "according to Stephen Krashen's input hypothesis." Grammatical skills are not even mentioned in the passage, so answer C is not supported by the passage.

Question 4 refers to the following passage.

"All knowledge that is about human society, and not about the natural world, is historical knowledge, and therefore rests upon judgment and interpretation. This is not to say that facts or data are non-existent, but that facts get their importance from what is made of them in interpretation, for interpretations depend very much on who the interpreter is, who he or she is addressing, what his or her purpose is, and at what historical moment the interpretation takes place" (Excerpt from *Culture and Imperialism,* Edward Said).

4. The author's primary purpose is to:

    A. assert that historical knowledge diverges from knowledge about nature.

    B. emphasize the historical significance of facts and data.

C. argue that historical knowledge hinges on analyses and opinions.

D. point out that historical knowledge is dubious from an academic perspective.

You may see questions on the ASVAB that ask about the author's purpose, tone, or attitude. Questions 4, 5, and 6 ask you about the author's purpose, attitude, and tone. For these types of questions, pay special attention to the first sentence of the passage and avoid answer choices that are overgeneralizations.

Tips and Explanations:

4. The correct answer is C.

   In the first sentence, the author states that "historical knowledge [. . .] rests upon judgment and interpretation. [. . .] Facts get their importance from what is made of them in interpretation." Interpretation is based on how something is analyzed, as well as the viewpoint of the interpreter. So, the author's purpose is to assert that historical knowledge hinges on analyses and opinions.

Question 5 refers to the following passage.

Recent research shows that social media platforms may actually be making us antisocial. Survey results indicate that many people would prefer to interact on Facebook or Twitter, rather than see friends and family in person. The primary reason cited for this phenomenon was that one does not need to go to the effort to dress up and travel in order to use these social media platforms.

Another independent survey revealed that people often remain glued to their hand-held devices to check their social media when they do go out with friends. It seems that social media platforms may be having a detrimental impact upon our social skills and interpersonal relationships.

5. The author would most likely agree with which of the following statements?

    A. Users of social media should go out more often.

    B. Users of social media should obtain a wider circle of friends.

    C. Users of social media should see family members only in person.

    D. Users of social media should turn off their hand-held devices when they are out with friends.

Tips and Explanations:

5. The correct answer is D.

    The author would most likely agree with the statement that users of social media turn off their hand-held devices when they are out with friends. The author points out that a "survey revealed that people often remain glued to their hand-held devices to check their social media when they do go out with friends."

Question 6 refers to the following passage.

"Celebrity" is the term used to describe someone who is famous and attracts attention from the general public and the world's media. Traditionally, a celebrity would gain the title by his or her work or achievements in a particular field of expertise. Actors, musicians, politicians, and inventors have all become celebrities in the past. However, as the twenty-first century progresses, a new celebrity has arrived – the nobody. As one peruses glossy TV magazines, it is easy to notice the amount of reality shows that now dominate our screens – Wife Swap, American Idol,

America's Got Talent, and the reality pioneer Big Brother. The concept itself of Big Brother is everything that George Orwell warned us about: "normal" people are thrust into the limelight to be mocked, glorified, vilified, and humiliated in equal measures. And we lap it up.

6. The writer's tone indicates that he believes that:

   A. reality TV participants are so-called celebrities who have no real achievements or expertise.

   B. reality TV participants are foolish for wanting to appear on television.

   C. the general public needs to stop watching reality TV shows in order to prevent the phenomenon of spurious celebrity.

   D. glossy TV magazines should stop promoting reality TV shows.

Tips and Explanations:

6. The correct answer is A.

   The author states that "traditionally, a celebrity would gain the title by his or her work or achievements in a particular field of expertise. [. . .] However, as the twenty-first century progresses, a new celebrity has arrived – the nobody." From these statements we can conclude that the writer's tone laments the fact that celebrities nowadays have no real achievements or expertise.

Questions 7 and 8 refer to the following passage.

Although there are many different types and sizes of coins in various countries, vending machines around the world operate on the same basic principles. The first check is the slot: coins that are bent or too large will not go in. Once inside the machine, coins fall into a cradle which weighs them. If a coin is too light, it is rejected and returned to the customer. Coins that pass the weight test are then passed along a runway beside a magnet. Electricity passes through the magnet, causing the coin to slow down in some cases. If the coin begins to slow down, its metallurgic composition has been deemed to be correct. The coin's slow speed causes it to miss the next obstacle, the deflector. Instead, the coin falls into the "accept" channel and the customer receives the product.

7. The last step in testing the coin is:

    A. the slot

    B. determination of metallurgic composition

    C. the accept channel

    D. the deflector

8. Based on the information in the passage, how is the metallurgical composition of a coin determined to be correct?

    A. by its weight

    B. by its increased velocity in the runway

    C. by whether it runs alongside the magnet

    D. by the electricity that has passed through the magnet

Question 7 is another type of a "specific detail" question. For this type of question, you will need to be able to identify the correct sequence of steps in a process. You will need to look at the passage carefully because the steps will not be carried out in the order that they are stated in the passage. So, pay special attention to timing and sequence words such as "if," "once," "before," and "instead."

Tips and Explanations:

7. The correct answer is B.

    The last step in testing the coin is the determination of its metallurgic composition. This step is provided in the sixth sentence of the paragraph: "If the coin begins to slow down, its metallurgic composition has been deemed to be correct." Be careful if you chose answer D. The deflector is not a step in the testing process, but rather an alternative outcome of the test.

8. The correct answer is D.

    The metallurgical composition of a coin is determined to be correct by the electricity that has passed through the magnet. The paragraph states: "Electricity passes through the magnet, causing the coin to slow down in some cases. If the coin begins to slow down, its metallurgic composition has been deemed to be correct." That is to say, the coin slows down because of the electricity that has passed through the magnet.

Questions 9 to 12 refer to the following passage.

Research shows that the rise in teenage smoking over the last ten years took place primarily in youth from more affluent families, in other words, families in which both parents were working and earning good incomes. Therefore, these teenagers were not from disadvantaged homes, as most people seemed to believe.

The facts demonstrate quite the opposite because the most striking and precipitous rise in smoking has been for teenagers from the most financially advantageous backgrounds. Furthermore, because of various lawsuits against the major tobacco companies, the price of cigarettes has actually declined sharply over the past decade. The paradox is that the increased demand for cigarettes originated from new teenage smokers who were from well-off families. Yet, contrary to these market forces, the price of tobacco products fell during this time.

9. Which of the following can be inferred from the passage?

    A. The majority of new teenage smokers in the last ten years could have afforded to pay higher prices for tobacco.

    B. Parents of affluent families are often not aware of the smoking habits of their children.

    C. Smoking among teenagers from disadvantaged homes also increased during the past decade.

    D. Major tobacco companies have recently faced bankruptcy.

10. From the information in the passage, it is reasonable to assume that:

    A. teenagers from affluent families smoke more than teenagers from disadvantaged homes.

    B. the price of tobacco products is normally unrelated to market forces.

    C. the price of cigarettes has fallen more than expected during the last ten years.

    D. contrary to popular belief, the rise in teenage smoking during the last ten years has been attributable to youth from wealthy family backgrounds.

Questions 9 and 10 ask you to make inferences from the passage. For these types of questions, you may be asked "what can be inferred" or "what can be assumed" from the information in the passage. For questions on inferences, look for words and phrases in the passage that express the writer's viewpoint.

Tips and Explanations:

9. The correct answer is A.

   Look for words and phrases in the passage that express the writer's viewpoint. See the phrase "contrary to these market forces" in the last sentence of the passage. The market forces refer to the factors that would have caused the price of tobacco to increase. Based on the word "contrary," it seems safe to conclude that the majority of new teenage smokers in the last ten years could have afforded to pay higher prices for tobacco, but in spite of this fact, the price did not go up.

10. The correct answer is D.

    The passage states that there has been a recent misconception about teenage smoking and that the price of tobacco should have gone up because youngsters from wealthy families could have afforded to pay a higher price. The following statement is the best assumption to draw from the passage because it mentions the misconception, as well as the pricing aspect: "Contrary to popular belief, the rise in teenage smoking in the last ten years has been attributable to youth from wealthy family backgrounds." So, answer D is the most accurate assumption.

The following question is an example of understanding words within the context of a passage. For questions on the meaning of words, you need to look for other words in the passage that are synonyms for the word in the question.

11. Which of the following is the best meaning of the word precipitous as it is used in this passage?

   A. dramatic

   B. unbelievable

   C. predictable

   D. dangerous

12. What is the author's primary purpose?

   A. to provide information on a recent trend

   B. to emphasize the dangers of smoking

   C. to dispel a common misconception

   D. to highlight the difference between two types of teenagers

Tips and Explanations:

11. The correct answer is A.

    Look for other words in the passage that are synonyms for the word in the question. "Dramatic" and "precipitous" are synonyms in the context of this passage. The word "striking" from the first sentence of the second paragraph of the passage is also a synonym for "precipitous."

12. The correct answer is C.

    In order to determine the author's purpose, you need to pay special attention to the last sentence of the first paragraph of a selection. This is where the writer normally puts his or her thesis statement, which is the author's main assertion or primary purpose. Looking at the last sentence of the first paragraph, we can see that the primary purpose of this passage is to dispel a common misconception. The idea of a misconception is indicated in the phrase "as most people seemed to believe" from the last sentence of the first paragraph.

Questions 13 to 15 refer to the following passage.

In December of 1880, a friend who was a veterinary surgeon gave Louis Pasteur two rabid dogs for research purposes. Victims of bites from rabid dogs normally showed no symptoms for three to twelve weeks. By then, however, the patient would be suffering from convulsions and delirium, and it would be too late to administer any remedy.

So-called treatments at that time consisted of burning the bitten area of skin with red-hot pokers or with carbolic acid. Pasteur devoted himself to discovering a more humane and effective method of treatment for the disease. His tests on the rabid dogs confirmed that rabies germs were isolated in the saliva and nervous systems of the animals. After many weeks of tests and experiments, Pasteur cultivated a vaccine. Derived from a weakened form of the rabies virus itself, the vaccine is administered before the microorganism is encountered and stimulates the immune system to recognize and fight off any future exposure to the organism.

13. In can be inferred from the passage that patients today would most likely respond to the prospect of treatments that were used in the past with:

    A. fear
    B. bewilderment
    C. scorn
    D. apathy

14. The primary purpose of the passage is to discuss:

    A. pasteurization and the rabies vaccine.

    B. the life and work of Louis Pasteur.

    C. Pasteur's discovery of the rabies vaccine.

    D. experimental research on rabid dogs.

15. The passage suggests that the discovery of the rabies vaccine was significant for which of the following reasons?

    A. It prevented animals from suffering during scientific experiments.

    B. It helped many people avoid physical suffering and death.

    C. It caused the treatments for other diseases to become more humane and effective.

    D. It contributed to the prevention of the contagions in germs, in general.

> Questions 13 to 15 provide additional practice with making inferences, understanding the author's purpose, and finding specific details within a passage.

Tips and Explanations:

13. The correct answer is A.

    It can be inferred that patients today would most likely respond to treatments of the past with fear. We can assume that burning the skin was feared because it is described as a "so-called" treatment. In addition, the second sentence of paragraph 2 implies that these treatments were inhumane.

14. The correct answer is C.

The primary purpose of the passage is to discuss Pasteur's discovery of the rabies vaccine. Paragraph 1 focuses on Pasteur's research on rabies. Paragraph 2 describes how the discovery of the rabies vaccine was made.

15. The correct answer is B.

The passage suggests that the discovery of the rabies vaccine was significant because it helped many people avoid physical suffering and death. We know this because paragraph 1 explains that patients with rabies would suffer from "convulsions and delirium, and it would be too late to administer any remedy." The phrase "too late to administer any remedy" indicates that the patient would die from the infection.

ASVAB Paragraph Comprehension – Practice Test 2

Question 1 refers to the following passage.

[1] The elements that constitute a liberal arts education have changed over the years. [2] The concept of liberal arts education is believed to have been established in ancient Greece. [3] Including the disciplines of logic, rhetoric, and grammar, a liberal arts education in those days was designed to train members of society to undertake important civic duties, such as jury service and public debate. [4] In modern parlance, the term "liberal arts education" can be interpreted in a variety of ways, although it is generally taken to mean that the studies will include courses in one or more of the subject areas of the humanities, such as languages, literature, or philosophy.

1. Which sentence from the passage best expresses the main idea?

    A. Sentence 1

    B. Sentence 2

    C. Sentence 3

    D. Sentence 4

Question 2 refers to the following passage.

Ludwig von Beethoven was one of the most influential figures in the development of musical forms during the Classical period. Born in Bonn, Germany, the composer became a professional musician before the age of 12. After studying under both Mozart and Haydn, Beethoven became a virtuoso pianist and had many wealthy patrons, who supported him financially. His most popular works are considered to be his fifth and sixth symphonies, and his only opera is entitled *Fidelio*. It is generally agreed that his compositions express the creative energy of the artist himself, rather than being written to suit the demands of his patrons.

2. The main purpose of the passage is to:

    A. suggest that the works of Beethoven, Mozart, and Haydn are very similar.

    B. explore the development of musical composition during the Classical period.

    C. provide background information about Beethoven's life and work.

    D. explain how Beethoven acquired many wealthy patrons.

Question 3 refers to the following passage.

For every building that is successfully constructed, there are countless others that have never received the chance to leave the drawing board. Some of these unbuilt structures were practical and mundane, while others expressed the flights of fancy of the architect. Known to us today only through the plans left on paper, many unbuilt buildings were originally designed to commemorate particular people or events. Such was the case with the monument dubbed the *Beacon of Progress*, which was to be erected in Chicago to display exhibits dedicated to great Americans in history. However, other proposed projects were far more quixotic, like that of *The Floating Spheres*, described as modules held aloft by hot air to house cities of the future.

3. Which of the following explains why some proposed projects were never constructed?

    A. Some projects were never undertaken due to the fact that they did not commemorate any significant event.

    B. The plans for some projects had serious design flaws.

    C. Some projects were too extravagant and impractical ever to be built.

    D. People were not ready to face the future of housing at the time that the construction of *The Floating Spheres* was proposed.

Question 4 refers to the following passage.

The ancient legal code of Babylonia had severe sanctions for a wide range of crimes. Perhaps best viewed as a way to express personal vengeance, punishments included cutting off the fingers of boys who had hit their fathers or gouging out the eyes of those who had blinded another person. As with most ancient peoples, the Babylonians did not believe in humane treatments for offenders. Sumerian King Ur Nammu, who formulated a set of laws that were surprisingly modern in their approach, did not follow these severe forms of retribution. Sumerian law stipulated that perpetrators of violent crimes pay monetary damages to their victims, and Ur Nammu's system is the first recorded example of financial awards being imposed in lieu of other forms of punishment.

4. The author mentions Sumerian King Ur Nammu primarily in order to:

   A. criticize previous Babylonian rulers.

   B. emphasize the severity of the Babylonian system of justice.

   C. imply that Babylonian sanctions were fair for their time.

   D. provide a contrast with the forms of punishment used by the Babylonians.

Question 5 refers to the following passage.

Painted by the Norwegian artist Edvard Munch, *The Scream* depicts the skeletal face of a person in clear psychological distress. Contrasted against a serene background of red and yellow swirls that represent the sunset, the desperation in the face illustrated in the painting is said to express humanity's reaction to the anxieties of modern life. Completing the work at the age of 29, Munch admitted that he felt as if a scream when through himself during that time since he was in a state of poor mental and physical health while painting the piece.

5. According to the passage, which one of the following factors most influenced Munch's painting of *The Scream*?

   A. his age at the time of working on the painting

   B. his own lack of personal well-being

   C. humanity's experiences of the anxieties of modern life

   D. the colors of the sunset

Questions 6 to 8 refer to the following passage.

Equating the whole history of the struggle of humankind to that of the class struggle, the social and political writings of Karl Marx have been the impetus of a great deal of change within society. According to Marxism, the political school of thought based on Marx's doctrines, the working class should strive to defeat capitalism, since capitalistic societies inherently have within them a dynamic that results in the wealthy ruling classes oppressing the masses. The nation state is seen as an instrument of class rule because it supports private capital and suppresses the common person through economic mechanisms, such as the taxation of wages. Because growth of private capital is stimulated by earning profits and extracting surplus value in the production process, wages have to be kept low.

Since capitalism reduces the purchasing power of workers to consume the goods that they produce, Marx emphasized that capitalism inheres in a central contradiction. Under the tenets of Marxism, capitalism is therefore inherently unstable. Marx asserted that productive power ideally should be in the hands of the general public, which would cause class differences to vanish. These idealistic writings have had a huge impact on culture and politics; yet, many believe that Marx's work lacked the practical details needed to bring about the changes to the class structure that he envisaged.

6. The author's primary purpose in the first paragraph is to:

    A. discuss why the writings of Karl Marx have had such enduring social and political importance.

B. explain the basic tenets of Marxism, before going on to discuss Marxist views on capitalism and the consequences of private capital.

C. critique the existing class structure and oppression of the masses.

D. decry the manner in which taxation and earning profits cause wages to be lowered.

7. Which of the following best describes the main points from each of the two paragraphs of the passage?

A. The first paragraph states an assertion, while the second paragraph refutes that assertion with statistical evidence.

B. The first paragraph explains a long-standing problem, and the second paragraph provides the potential solution.

C. The first paragraph introduces and expounds upon a theory, while the second paragraph points out criticisms of the theory.

D. The first paragraph gives the background to the topic in a general way, and the second paragraph provides specific details about the topic.

8. The writer mentions the "huge impact" that these writings have had on culture and politics in the last sentence in order to:

A. contrast this impact to Marx's failure to include practical instructions in his work.

B. highlight the way in which capitalism is often unstable.

C. reiterate the importance of giving power back to the general populace.

D. underscore the fact that class differences have not yet vanished.

Questions 9 to 11 refer to the following passage.

In Southern Spain and France, Stone Age artists painted stunning drawings on the walls of caves nearly 30,000 years ago. Painting pictures of the animals upon which they relied for food, the artists worked by the faint light of lamps that were made of animal fat and twigs.

In addition to having to work in relative darkness, the artists had to endure great physical discomfort since the inner chambers of the caves were sometimes less than three feet in height. Thus, the artists were required to crouch or squat uncomfortably as they practiced their craft.

Their paints were mixed from natural elements such as yellow ochre, clay, calcium carbonate, and iron oxide. However, many other natural elements and minerals were not used. An analysis of the cave paintings reveals that the colors of the paints used by the artists ranged from light yellow to dark black.

The artists utilized ochre and manganese as engraving tools in order first to etch their outlines on the walls of the caves. Before removing their lamps and leaving their creations to dry, they painted the walls with brushes of animal hair or feathers. Archeologists have also discovered that ladders and scaffolding were used in higher areas of the caves.

9. What was the last step in the process of Stone Age cave drawings?

    A. The paintings were etched.

    B. The paint was applied.

C. The lamps were removed.

D. The artwork was left to dry.

10. Which of the following best expresses the attitude of the writer?

A. It is surprising that the tools of Stone Age artists were similar to those that artists use today.

B. It is amazing that Stone Age artists were able to paint such beautiful creations in spite of the extreme conditions they faced.

C. The lack of light in the caves had an effect on their esthetic quality.

D. It is predictable and banal that Stone Age artists would paint pictures of animals.

11. Which sentence least supports the main idea of the passage?

A. Thus, the artists were required to crouch or squat uncomfortably as they practiced their craft.

B. Their paints were mixed from natural elements such as yellow ochre, clay, calcium carbonate, and iron oxide.

C. However, many other natural elements and minerals were not used.

D. An analysis of the cave paintings reveals that the colors of the paints used by the artists ranged from light yellow to dark black.

Questions 12 to 15 refer to the following passage.

Working in a run-down laboratory near Paris, Marie Curie worked around the clock to discover a radioactive element. When she finally captured her quarry in 1902, she named it "radium" after the Latin word meaning ray.

Madame Curie should certainly be an inspiration to scientists today. She had spent the day blending chemical compounds which could be used to destroy unhealthy cells in the body. As she was about to retire to bed that evening, she decided to return to her lab. There she found that the chemical compound had become crystalized in the bowls and was emitting the elusive light that she sought.

Inspired by the French scientist Henri Becquerel, Curie won the Nobel Prize for Chemistry in 1903. Upon winning the prize, she declared that the radioactive element would be used only to treat disease and would not be used for commercial profit.

Today radium provides an effective remedy for certain types of cancer. Radium, now used for a treatment called radiotherapy, works by inundating diseased cells with radioactive particles. Its success lies in the fact that it eradicates malignant cells without any lasting ill effects on the body.

12. Which of the following is the best meaning of the word quarry as it is used in this passage?

   A. a precious commodity

   B. an unknown catalyst

   C. an object that is sought

   D. a chemical compound

13. According to the information in the passage, why is radium treatment used as a cancer therapy?

    A. because it is cost effective

    B. because it destroys cancerous cells

    C. because it has no long-term effects

    D. because it emits a glowing light

14. What is the most appropriate title of the passage?

    A. Madame Curie: An Inventive Chemist

    B. The Discoveries of Madame Curie

    C. The Use of Radium to Treat Cancer

    D. The Discovery and Use of Radium

15. Which of the following phrases or sentences from the passage best expresses the opinion of the author?

    A. Marie Curie worked around the clock to discover a radioactive element.

    B. Madame Curie should certainly be an inspiration to scientists today.

    C. She had spent the day blending chemical compounds which could be used to destroy unhealthy cells in the body.

    D. Upon winning the prize, she declared that the radioactive element would be used only to treat disease and would not be used for commercial profit.

Reading Practice Test 2 – Explanations for the Answers

1. The correct answer is A. The time span in the passage is from ancient Greece to the modern day, so the main idea of the passage is summed up in the statement that "the elements that constitute a liberal arts education have changed over the years."

2. The correct answer is C. The primary purpose of the passage is to provide background information about Beethoven's life and work. The passage begins by providing information about the composer's musical training, before going on to talk about his professional life and compositions.

3. The correct answer is C. Some proposed projects were never constructed because they were too extravagant and impractical ever to be built. The passage states: "other proposed projects were far more quixotic." The word "quixotic" means extravagant and impractical.

4. The correct answer is D. The author mentions Sumerian King Ur Nammu primarily in order to provide a contrast with the usual forms of punishment used by the Babylonians. The passage states that "the Babylonians did not believe in humane treatments for offenders." However, King Ur Nammu "did not follow these severe forms of retribution."

5. The correct answer is B. Munch's own lack of personal well-being most influenced his painting of *The Scream*. The last sentence of the passage explains that "Munch admitted that he felt as if a scream when through himself during that time since he was in a state of poor mental and physical health while painting the piece."

6. The correct answer is B. The author's primary purpose in the first paragraph is to explain the basic tenets of Marxism, before going on to discuss Marxist views on capitalism and the consequences of private capital. We know this because the second sentence begins with the phrase "according to Marxism." Answer A is too general, and answers C and D are too specific.

7. The correct answer is D. The first paragraph gives the background to the topic in a general way, and the second paragraph provides specific details about the topic. You may be tempted to choose answer C, but the criticism is only one aspect of the information provided in paragraph 2.

8. The correct answer is A. The writer mentions the "huge impact" that these writings have had on culture and politics in the last sentence in order to contrast this impact to Marx's failure to include practical instructions in his work. We know that the author is making a comparison or contrast because the sentence includes with the word "yet."

9. The correct answer is D. We need to have a look at the first and second sentences of the last paragraph, which state: "The artists utilized ochre and manganese as engraving tools in order first to etch their outlines on the walls of the caves. Before removing their lamps and leaving their creations to dry, they painted the walls with brushes of animal hair or feathers." Be sure to read sentences like this one very carefully. The etching is the first step. The application of the paint is the second step. Removing the lamps is the third step, while leaving the paint to dry is the final step.

10. The correct answer is B. The attitude of the writer is that it is amazing that Stone Age artists were able to paint such beautiful creations in spite of the extreme conditions they faced. For questions like this one, look for adjectives in the passage that give hints about the author's point of view. The phrase "stunning drawings" in paragraph one indicates the author's amazement.

11. The correct answer is C. The article focuses on the natural elements that were used in the process of creating the drawings. The passage is therefore not concerned with other natural elements that were not used.

12. The correct answer is C. For vocabulary questions like this one, you need to bear in mind that the word provided will have different interpretations, depending on its context. "Quarry" can mean a hole in which one digs for rock. Alternatively, "quarry" can refer to something that is hunted or pursued. Also remember that for vocabulary questions, you need to look for synonyms in the passage. In sentence one, we see the word "discover." In the last sentence of paragraph two, we see the phrase "the elusive light that she sought." Therefore, we can surmise that "quarry" is something one wants to discover or an object being sought.

13. The correct answer is B. Questions like this will have distractor answers which will reiterate phrases from the passage, although these phrases do not answer the question. We know that answer B is correct because the final sentence of the passage states: "Its success lies in the fact that it eradicates malignant cells without any lasting ill effects on the body." You may be tempted to choose answer C. However, answer C is too general since radium has long-term positive effects [i.e., destroying malignant cells] without having any long-term negative effects.

14. The correct answer is D. For main idea questions, as well as for questions on selecting a title for a selection, you will need to choose an answer that is neither too general nor too specific. Answers A and B are much too general since the passage does not focus on the entire life and work of Madame Curie. Answer C is too specific because cancer treatment is mentioned in only the last paragraph. Therefore, "The Discovery and Use of Radium" is the best title for the passage.

15. The correct answer is B. For "opinion vs. fact" questions, look for modal verbs (should, would, may, might) and superlative adjectives that express opinions (the best, the most, etc). The notion whether someone should be an inspiration to others is a matter of personal opinion, so B is the best answer.

ASVAB Paragraph Comprehension – Practice Test 3

Question 1 refers to the following passage.

Depicting the events of a single day, James Joyce's epic novel *Ulysses* took more than 20,000 hours, or a total of eight years, to write. Set in Dublin, the novel was initially published in installments as a series before the Parisian publishing house Shakespeare and Company issued a limited edition of 1,000 copies. The book was risqué for its time, and was classified as obscene material in the United Stated. After the work was cleared of obscenity charges, an unexpurgated version was accepted for publication by Random House in New York. Ironically, it was not available in Dublin until 40 years later.

1. The passage implies which of the following about the fact that *Ulysses* was published in Dublin 40 years after it was released in New York?

    A. Irish publishing companies often engage in dilatory practices when dealing with their authors.

    B. Irish publishers were dissuaded in publishing the novel since it depicted the events of only one day.

    C. Random House did not have a division in Dublin at that time.

    D Morals of behavior in Dublin were much stricter than those of the United States at that time.

Question 2 refers to the following passage.

Although the foundations of the movement can be traced back to the artists van Gogh and Gauguin in the late nineteenth century, the first recorded use of the term Expressionism was in Germany in the early twentieth century. Influencing art, literature, theater, and architecture, Expressionism strives to illustrate the inner emotional reaction to a reality. In this approach, the traditional notion of realism is to be disregarded, as are the conventional ideas of beauty and proportion. Accordingly, Expressionist artists use distortion, incongruous color schemes, and exaggerated shapes and sizes to reveal their emotions. The impact of the movement is also present in fictional and poetic works of the era, particularly those which represent the dislocation of the individual within society.

2. According to the passage, which one of the following phenomena is true?

   A. Artistic movements are ever-changing with the passage of time.

   B. Abstract art is more popular than realistic art.

   C. Human beings felt out of sync with their communities at the time Expressionism was taking place.

   D. Most twentieth century artists were nonconventional.

Question 3 refers to the following passage.

The Higgs mechanism is the process in quantum field theory whereby symmetry is broken down, leading to massive particles. Quantum field theory alone tells us that all particles should be massless. Yet, groundbreaking scientific research has found that particles can acquire mass when the symmetry of energy within a system is less than that of the interaction governing the system. Theoretically, scientists understand that the Higgs particle is a by-product of the acquisition of mass by other particles. Discovering this elusive particle remains one of the greatest challenges of modern-day particle physicists.

3. The author most likely elaborates on quantum field theory in the second sentence in order to:

   A. change the subject from mechanisms to particles.

   B. reveal that the Higgs mechanism inheres in a basic contradiction.

   C. illustrate how the symmetry of energy within a system can be lower than that of the governing system.

   D. explain the process by which massive particles are formed.

Question 4 refers to the following passage.

[1] Reconstruction is the process whereby words are constructed in an undocumented language by comparing its sound system to those of known related languages. [2] The practice, which is also called internal reconstruction, is based on the postulation that certain sounds have variants in other languages. [3] For instance, the Latin word *pater* and the Gothic word *fadar* show a systematic correspondence between the *p* and *f* sounds in these languages. [4] The practice of reconstruction leads to the conclusion that *p* was the earlier variant of the *f* consonant in other related languages, as well as in antediluvian languages and Indo-European forms.

4. Which sentence from the passage best reflects its main idea?

    A. Sentence 1

    B. Sentence 2

    C. Sentence 3

    D. Sentence 4

Question 5 refers to the following passage.

There has been a fundamental change in the relationship between the actor and the audience in recent years. According to Aristotelian principles, actors should provoke an emotional catharsis in the members of the audience. Traditionally, actors have provided this emotional release, but this is far from the case in the performances in many modern motion pictures and television programs. Even though many productions are increasingly based on contrived stories or weak plots, modern actors could do more with these roles than merely create mindless diversions. Sadly, many performers nowadays lack gravitas. When actors engage in such vacuous performances, they do not even begin to serve the higher purpose of their profession.

5. According to the passage, one way to distinguish a traditional actor from a modern one is by considering:

    A. the seriousness of the subject matter of the production.

    B. the emotional response of the viewers.

    C. the strength of the plot.

    D. the originality of the storyline.

Questions 6 and 7 refer to the following passage.

Known as the Centennial State, Colorado is divided into sixty-three counties. The eastern part of the state was gained by the U.S. in 1803 as part of the Louisiana Purchase, while the western part was acquired from Mexico by treaty in 1848. Colorado joined the union as the 38th state in 1876, shortly after the first substantial discovery of gold in the state near Pikes Peak in 1859.

Today, commerce in the state involves the production of wheat, hay, corn, sugar beets, and other crops, as well as cattle ranching and raising other livestock. The packaging, processing, fabrication, and defense industries form the lion's share of revenues from business in the state. Perhaps lesser-known is the fact that Colorado contains the world's largest deposits of molybdenum, a brittle silver-grey metallic chemical element that is used in some alloy steels.

6. Which of the following is the best meaning of the phrase "lion's share of" in the second paragraph?

   A. majority of

   B. superfluous for

   C. excessive with

   D. abundant by

7. The primary purpose of the passage is to:

   A. discuss trade and commerce in a particular state.

   B. sum up the historical background and notable features of a particular state.

   C. provide pertinent political details about the acquisition of a particular state.

   D. emphasize the importance of agriculture for trade and commerce in Colorado.

Questions 8 to 11 refer to the following passage.

In his book *Il Milione*, known in English as *The Travels of Marco Polo*, the intrepid explorer describes the marvels he encountered as he journeyed to China. Upon his visit to the emperor Kublai Khan in Cathay, Polo witnessed magical illusions performed by the court wizards of the supreme ruler. Watching in amazement as the wizards recited incantations, Polo first saw a row of golden cups <u>levitate</u> over the table as Khan drank from each one without spilling a drop. Polo also recounted that Khan had astonishing powers over wild animals. Unrestrained and ostensibly obedient, lions would appear to lie down in humility in front of the emperor.

However, Khan was venerated for much more than these acts of mere wizardry. Polo's account tells us that the ruler presided over an extremely modern state, which had paper currency, a vast postal system, and a network of well-maintained roadways. Although some have disputed the veracity of Polo's written account of the Khan Empire, common sense tells us that there would have been little motive for the explorer to have exaggerated his version of events since he was being held captive at the time with no hope of release.

8. It can be inferred from the passage that the primary reason why the court wizards performed magical illusions was to:

   A. venerate the majesty of Kublai Khan.

   B. play a trick on Marco Polo.

   C. provide an interesting story for the book *Il Milione*.

   D. make Kublai Khan and his court appear powerful and mysterious.

9. The author uses the word "levitate" in paragraph 1 to mean:

   A. rise

   B. drag

   C. hover

   D. linger

10. Some people find fault with *Il Milione* because:

    A. Marco Polo's account goes against common sense.

    B. paper currency did not really exist during Khan's rule.

    C. Khan's state was not as modern as Polo described.

    D. it is unclear whether we should believe Polo's version of events.

11. Which of the following is the best title for the passage?

    A. Marco Polo: The Intrepid Traveler

    B. Facts about "Il Milione: The Travels of Marco Polo"

    C. Marco Polo's Marvelous Journey to China

    D. Kublai Khan and His Acts of Wizardry

Questions 12 to 15 refer to the following passage.

A complex series of interactive patterns govern nearly everything the human body does. We eat to a rhythm and drink, sleep, and even breathe to separate ones. Research shows that the human body clock is affected by three main rhythmic cycles: the rhythm at which the earth revolves on its axis, the monthly revolution of the moon around the earth, and the annual revolution of the earth around the sun. These rhythms create a sense of time that is both physiological as well as mental. Humans feel hungry about every four hours, sleep about eight hours in every twenty-four-hour period, and dream in cycles of approximately ninety minutes each.

These natural rhythms, sometimes called circadian rhythms, are partially controlled by the hypothalamus in the brain. Circadian rhythms help to explain the "lark vs. owl" hypothesis. Larks are those who quite rightly prefer to rise early in the morning and go to bed early, while owls are those who feel at their best at night and stay up too late. *These cycles* explain the phenomenon of jet lag, when the individual's body clock is out of step with the actual clock time in his or her new location in the world. In humans, births and deaths also follow predictable cycles, with most births and deaths occurring between midnight and 6:00 a.m.

12. The main idea of the passage is that:

    A. circadian rhythms govern various bodily functions and processes.

    B. circadian rhythms are both physiological and mental.

    C. circadian rhythms help to explain the "lark vs. owl" hypothesis.

    D. we drink, sleep, and even breathe to circadian rhythms.

13. According to the passage, circadian rhythms are controlled by:

    A. the "lark vs. owl" hypothesis

    B. the hypothalamus in the brain

    C. the individual's body clock

    D. cycles of birth and death

14. The author's attitude toward owls in the "lark vs. owl" hypothesis can best be described as one of:

    A. disapproval

    B. skepticism

    C. hostility

    D. support

15. From the passage, it is reasonable to assume that sufferers of jet lag should do which of the following?

    A. Better control their circadian rhythms.

    B. Take medicine to regulate the hypothalamus.

    C. Go to bed earlier than usual.

    D. Allow their body clocks to adjust to the time difference naturally.

Reading Practice Test 3 – Explanations for the Answers

1. The correct answer is D. The passage implies that morals of behavior in Dublin were much stricter than those of the United States at the time that *Ulysses* was published in New York. The passage tells us that "the book was risqué for its time" and was originally classified as "obscene material". Note that the word "risqué" means indecent.

2. The correct answer is C. The passage states that Expressionism illustrates the way in which human beings felt out of sync with their communities at the time this movement was taking place. The last sentence of the passage comments that Expressionism represents "the dislocation of the individual within society."

3. The correct answer is B. The author most likely mentions quantum field theory in order to reveal that the Higgs mechanism inheres in a basic contradiction. In other words, quantum field theory tells us that all particles should be massless, but the Higgs mechanism shows that particles can acquire mass.

4. The correct answer is A. The passage is describing the theory of language reconstruction, which is the topic of sentence 1. Sentences 2, 3, and 4 are too specific to be the main idea. Sentence 2 talks about the basis of the theory. Sentence 3 provides an example, while sentence 4 describes a conclusion.

5. The correct answer is B. According to the passage, one way to distinguish a traditional actor from a modern one is by considering the emotional response of the viewers. The passage explains: "Traditionally, actors have provided this emotional

release, but this is far from the case in the performances in many modern motion pictures and television programs."

6. The correct answer is A. The phrase "majority of" could be substituted for "lion's share of" in the second paragraph with no change in meaning. Both phrases refer to the largest part of something.

7. The correct answer is B. The primary purpose of the passage is to sum up the historical background and notable features of a particular state. The other answer choices provide specific details from the passage, rather than the primary purpose.

8. The correct answer is D. It can be inferred from the passage that the primary reason why the court wizards performed magical illusions was to make Kublai Khan and his court appear powerful and mysterious. The first paragraph uses the words "amazement" and "astonishing" to express the mysteriousness of the court.

9. The correct answer is C. The author uses the word "levitate" in paragraph 1 to mean hover. The words "levitate" and "hover" both mean to be suspended in midair.

10. The correct answer is D. Some find fault with *Il Milione* because it is unclear whether we believe Polo's version of events. The passage explains that "Although some have disputed the veracity of Polo's written account of the Khan Empire, common sense tells us that there would have been little motive for the explorer to have exaggerated his version of events." The phrase "dispute the veracity" means that they doubt whether the story is true.

11. The correct answer is B. Paragraph 1 describes the book *Il Milione*, and paragraph 2 provides some additional information about Polo's written account of events. So, the best title is Facts about "Il Milione: The Travels of Marco Polo"

12. The correct answer is A. The main idea of the passage is that circadian rhythms govern various bodily functions and processes.

13. The correct answer is B. According to the passage, circadian rhythms are controlled by the hypothalamus in the brain. The second paragraphs states: "These natural rhythms, sometimes called circadian rhythms, are partially controlled by the hypothalamus in the brain."

14. The correct answer is A. The author's attitude toward owls in the "lark vs. owl" hypothesis can best be described as one of disapproval. The author says that larks "quite rightly prefer to rise early in the morning," but owls "stay up too late." So, the author disapproves of the owl's behavior.

15. The correct answer is D. It is reasonable to assume that sufferers of jet lag allow their body clocks to adjust to the time difference naturally. The second paragraph begins by explaining that "these natural rhythms, sometimes called circadian rhythms, are partially controlled by the hypothalamus in the brain." Since the rhythms are referred to as a natural phenomenon, it is reasonable to assume that the time difference be overcome naturally.

ASVAB Paragraph Comprehension – Practice Test 4

Questions 1 to 3 refer to the following passage.

When will global oil supply start to diminish? An important part of the answer to this frequently-asked question comes down to oil field decline rates – that is, the annual rate at which production from existing fields goes down. In an effort to answer the question about the global decline rate, Cambridge Energy Research Associates (CERA) launched a detailed, in-depth research project.

When the CERA team analyzed recent production trends in its database, it found that the aggregate global decline rate for fields currently in production is approximately 4.5 percent per year. This is far lower than the 8 percent figure used in many studies. The 4.5 percent figure provides additional support for CERA's view that oil production capacity can grow enough over the next decade to meet the anticipated increase in demand. A key conclusion of the study is that there is no evidence that oilfield decline rates will increase suddenly. The study of decline rates allows for better and more reliable projections about future oil supply. The CERA study is a signpost that shows we are gaining a better understanding of below-ground factors, such as decline rates, that will shape the future of world oil supply.

1. What is the primary subject of this passage?

    A. Global oil supply has declined due to the concomitant oil field decline rate, but recent research shows that the decline rate is not as poor as previously thought.

B. Questions surrounding the decline in the global oil supply are worthy of investigation by independent bodies such as Cambridge Energy Research Associates.

C. Databases for trends in oil production have misstated figures recently, so the decline in the oil supply is not as low as expected.

D. Better and more reliable projections are needed in order to gain an understanding of below-ground factors such as decline rates.

2. Which of the following best explains the reason why Cambridge Energy Research Associates carried out their research project?

   A. to understand why below-ground factors had decreased

   B. to investigate oilfield decline rates

   C. to evaluate the links in the chain of the oil supply

   D. to have more information for their database

3. According to the text, why will oil production capacity be able to meet the anticipated increase in demand?

   A. because CERA has calculated a decline rate of 8 percent.

   B. because the CERA study has resulted in better and more reliable projections.

   C. because oilfield decline rates are not as bad as previously thought.

   D. because of below-ground factors.

Questions 4 and 5 refer to the following passage.

The phrase "cultural diversity" refers to the manifold ways in which the cultures of groups and societies find expression. These expressions are passed on within and among groups and societies. Cultural diversity is made manifest not only through the varied ways in which the cultural heritage of humanity is expressed and transmitted through cultural expression, but also through diverse modes of artistic creation. Therefore, cultural diversity is a rich asset for individuals and societies.

The protection, promotion, and maintenance of cultural diversity are essential requirements for sustainable development for the benefit of present and future generations. Equitable access to a rich and diversified range of cultural expressions from all over the world and access of cultures to the means of expressions and dissemination constitute important elements for enhancing cultural diversity and encouraging mutual understanding between and among nations.

4. The phrase "cultural diversity" primarily refers to:

    A. communication within groups and societies.

    B. modes of artistic production and creation.

    C. how groups and societies express their cultural heritages.

    D. the expression and augmentation of humanity.

5. The writer's main argument is that:

    A. cultural diversity is an important resource for individuals and societies.

    B. cultural diversity should be accessed and disseminated equitably.

C. cultural diversity is not sufficiently respected, protected, and promoted.

D. international cooperation is needed in order to strengthen cultural diversity.

Questions 6 to 10 refer to the following passage.

Today archaeologists are still endeavoring to uncover the secrets of Africa's past. Evidence of the earliest human activity has been found in the south and east of the continent, where climatic conditions helped to preserve the human skeletons and stone tools found there. Genetic science confirms that these are quite likely the oldest remains in the world of modern people, with this classification based on the ability of humans to become adaptable and ready to respond to environmental change. Even though the artifacts and skeletons of early Africans are most commonly found in a highly fragmented state, these findings are more than sufficient in order to make a number of significant conclusions.

Perhaps the most important discovery is that there is great <u>variation</u> among the human remains, indicating a wide array of physical differences among members of the population. While the early population was diverse, it has been well established that the earliest species of hominids spread from Africa to other continents. The first traces of human technology, consisting of simple stone tools, were also discovered in Africa. Having been developed long before the invention of metallurgy, tools had gradually become smaller and more sophisticated. Microliths, fine stone tools that were fitted to handles, were used as cutting and scraping tools and may even have been the precursor to the bow and arrow.

6. Which of the following best describes the author's purpose in this passage?

    A. A common fallacy is described, and then it is refuted.

    B. An unresolved question is posed, and then it is answered.

    C. A problem is described, and then a solution is discussed.

    D General information about the research is provided, and then the specific findings of the research are presented.

7. The author states that "genetic science confirms that these are quite likely the oldest remains in the world of modern people" in paragraph 1 primarily in order to emphasize:

    A. the depth and breadth of Africa's history.

    B. the way that climatic conditions can help to preserve skeletons.

    C. the importance of the stone tools found in African sites.

    D. the significance of archeological discoveries in Africa.

8. As used in paragraph 2, the word "variation" most likely means:

    A. distinction

    B. discrepancy

    C. variety

    D. changeability

9. From the passage, it can be inferred that some of the archeological discoveries from Africa:

   A. were broken into small pieces or extremely damaged.

   B. would not have been located without modern genetic science.

   C. were not as important as those from other continents.

   D. supported the development of metallurgy.

10. The passage suggests that the discovery of microliths was significant for which one of the following reasons?

    A. Microliths illustrate the importance of the invention of the bow and arrow.

    B. Microliths demonstrate the level of sophistication and ingenuity of the prehistoric African population.

    C. Microliths support the view that hominids spread to other continents.

    D. Microliths show that technology at that time consisted of more than stone tools.

Question 11 refers to the following passage.

In the small hours of September 17, 1949, Constables Ronald Anderson and Warren Shaddock hit Queen's Quay in Toronto just as the SS Noronic, the largest passenger ship on the Great Lakes, erupted into flames that shot up as high as the ship's masthead. The first to arrive, their police cruiser was surrounded by people in shock, many of them injured. A passenger alerted Anderson to the many wounded in the water and those standing on the decks, some of whom were on fire. Anderson stripped off his uniform and jumped into the frigid, oily water, dragging the injured back to the dock. From there, police officers hauled them up by rope, where Shaddock and others administered first aid. Detective Cyril Cole joined Anderson in the water, with both retrieving bodies and survivors. Later, fireboats arrived to assist. Many of the responding officers were World War II Veterans.

11. From the passage, it is reasonable to assume that:

    A. Anderson was the first man in the water.

    B. Toronto did not have an ambulance service at the time of the disaster.

    C. The press was an unwelcome intrusion at the site of the disaster.

    D. People stopped traveling by luxury ship on the Great Lakes after the disaster because they considered it too dangerous.

Questions 12 to 15 refer to the following passage.

Dance notation is to choreography what written scores are to music and what written scripts are to drama. The representation of movement in these notation systems varies, although most are based on drawings, stick figures, abbreviations, musical notes, or abstract symbols. Recording the movements of dance through a shortened series of characters or symbols, more than one hundred systems of dance notation have been created over the past few centuries.

In the seventeenth century, Pierre Beauchamp devised a notation system for Baroque dance. Known as Beauchamp-Feuillet notation, his system was used to record dances until the end of the eighteenth century. Later, Vladimir Ivanovich Stepanov, a Russian, was responsible for notating choreographic scores for the famous *Sergevev Ballet Collection*, including works such as *Swan Lake*, *Sleeping Beauty*, and *The Nutcracker*. Thanks to Stepanov's system, dance companies were enabled to stage these works outside of Russia. Hanva Holm was the first choreographer to copyright the notations of her dance scores, securing the rights for *Kiss Me Kate* in 1948. Two other notation systems, Labanotation and Benesh notation, also known as choreology, are in wide-spread use today. Apple created the first computerized system to display an animated figure on the screen that illustrated dance moves, and many other software systems have been developed to facilitate computerized dance notation.

12. The passage is primarily concerned with:

    A. describing the history of dance notation and its use.

    B. illustrating the way in which dance notation has improved performance.

    C. defending changes to various dance notation systems.

    D. criticizing outdated forms of dance notation.

13. According to the passage, Beauchamp-Feuillet notation differs from Vladimir Ivanovich Stepanov's notation system in that Stepanov's system:

    A. was used for a different type of dance during a different time period.

    B. was used for works performed in the Russian language.

    C. was never copyrighted.

    D. was also known as choreology.

14. The passage indicates which of the following about Hanva Holm?

    A. She was a Broadway dancer in her day.

    B. She performed as a dancer in *Kiss Me Kate* in 1948.

    C. She was the first person to register intellectual property rights for a dance notation system.

    D. Her system is still in widespread use today.

15. The author most likely mentions Apple and other computerized dance notation systems in the last sentence of the passage in order to:

    A. point out the similarities among various computerized systems.

    B. advocate the use of computer software for choreographed performances.

    C. identify the systems that have replaced choreology.

    D. indicate possible trends in dance notation.

Reading Practice Test 4 – Explanations for the Answers

1. The correct answer is A. In the first paragraph, the author discusses the reasons for the decline in the global oil supply. In the second paragraph, the author describes a research report which indicates that the oil supply will be sufficient for anticipated demand. So, the primary subject of the passage is that the global oil supply has declined due to the concomitant oil field decline rate, but recent research shows that the decline rate is not as poor as previously thought.

2. The correct answer is B. Cambridge Energy Research Associates carried out their research project in order to investigate oilfield decline rates. We can see this from the last sentence of the first paragraph.

3. The correct answer is C. This is an example of a question that asks you to look for a specific detail in the text. According to the text, oil production capacity will be able to meet the anticipated increase in demand because oilfield decline rates are not as bad as previously thought. Paragraph 2 states: when the CERA team analyzed recent production trends in its database, it found that the aggregate global decline rate for fields currently in production is approximately 4.5 percent per year. This is far lower than the 8 percent figure used by many studies. A decline (or loss) at a rate of 4.5% is better than a decline at a rate of 8%. Answer choice A is false according to the passage. Answer choices C and D contain specific information from the passage, but these answer choices do not answer the question.

4. The correct answer is C. The phrase "cultural diversity" primarily refers to how groups and societies express their cultural heritages. We can see this definition in

the first sentence of the passage, which states: "The phrase 'cultural diversity' refers to the manifold ways in which the cultures of groups and societies find expression."

5. The correct answer is A. The writer's main argument is that cultural diversity is an important resource for individuals and societies. We can see this from the following underlined words that the author uses in paragraph two of the text: "The <u>protection</u>, <u>promotion</u>, and <u>maintenance</u> of cultural diversity are <u>essential</u> requirements for sustainable development for the <u>benefit</u> of present and future generations. <u>Equitable</u> access to a rich and <u>diversified</u> range of cultural expressions from all over the world and access of cultures to the means of expressions and dissemination constitute <u>important</u> elements for <u>enhancing</u> cultural diversity and <u>encouraging</u> mutual understanding between and among nations."

6. The correct answer is D. General information about the research is provided, and then the specific findings of the research are presented. The first paragraph describes the background to archeological research in Africa, and the second paragraph gives specific details about the remains and artifacts that were discovered there.

7. The correct answer is D. The author states that "genetic science confirms that these are quite likely the oldest remains in the world of modern people" in paragraph 1 primarily in order to emphasize the significance of archeological discoveries in Africa. We know this because the paragraph goes on to explain that "these findings are more than sufficient in order to make a number of significant conclusions."

8. The correct answer is C. As used in paragraph 2, the word "variation" most likely means variety. "Variation" is synonymous with the words "wide array" and "diverse," which are used later in paragraph 2.

9. The correct answer is A. From the passage, it can be inferred that some of the archeological discoveries from Africa were broken into small pieces or extremely damaged. The last sentence of paragraph 1 of the passage tells us that "the artifacts and skeletons of early Africans are most commonly found in a highly fragmented state." "Fragmented" means broken into pieces.

10. The correct answer is B. The passage suggests that the discovery of microliths was significant because these tools demonstrate the level of sophistication and ingenuity of the prehistoric African population. The second to last sentence of paragraph 2 states: "Having been developed long before the invention of metallurgy, tools had gradually become smaller and more sophisticated." Microliths are then given as an example of more sophisticated tools.

11. The correct answer is A. This is an inference type of question. The writer states that Anderson and Shaddock were the first to arrive. We then read that Anderson got in the water, so we can make the small logical conclusion that Anderson was the first man in the water. Answers B, C, and D are not supported by the text.

12. The correct answer is A. The passage is primarily concerned with describing the history of dance notation and its use. The theme of the passage is introduced in the last sentence of the first paragraph, which says that "more than one hundred systems of dance notation have been created over the past few centuries." The phrase "past few centuries" indicates that a historical account is going to be given.

13. The correct answer is A. According to the passage, Beauchamp-Feuillet notation differs from Vladimir Ivanovich Stepanov's notation system in that Stepanov's system was used for a different type of dance during a different time period. Stepanov's system was used for ballet after the eighteenth century. The system that Pierre Beauchamp devised was used for Baroque dance until the end of the eighteenth century.

14. The correct answer is C. The passage indicates that Hanva Holm was the first person to register intellectual property rights for a dance notation system. Paragraph 2 states that "Hanva Holm was the first choreographer to copyright the notations of her dance scores." Copyright is a kind of intellectual property right.

15. The correct answer is D. The author most likely mentions Apple and other computerized dance notation systems in the last sentence of the passage in order to indicate possible trends in dance notation. We know this because the sentence focuses on new developments in dance notation.

ASVAB Paragraph Comprehension – Practice Test 5

Question 1 refers to the following passage.

Europeans could teach us a great deal in the matter of penology. They allow their prisoners more liberty; they show a more sympathetic interest in their welfare than we do. Everything is done to teach offenders industry and morality. As their behavior improves, they are given better food and various privileges. Everything and every prisoner is scrupulously clean. When considering the rising crime rates in the United States, where serving a prison sentence often leads to re-offending, one can readily see that this system of rehabilitation is more effective.

1. The writer's main purpose is to express which of the following objections to the prison system in the United States?

    A. It is unsympathetic.

    B. It is not efficacious.

    C. It is not clean.

    D. It is too restrictive.

Question 2 refers to the following passage.

Statistical reports show that most businesses spend more than $100 million just to build up and introduce a new consumer product in the United States. Hence, if a business does not have money at its incipience, it will be impossible for the business to grow. So, businesses that seek to develop products and technology may fail if they don't borrow the money to do so.

Generally, many business owners will run to their family, relatives, or friends to get financial backup or investment. Others would turn to financial institutions such as banks or lending companies. As much as these funding sources can help new projects, they may be inadequate, or businesses may be charged higher interest rates, which, in turn, will put a financial risk on a fledging business. For this reason, the US government offers financial help to businesses seeking to develop new products or technology. Government grants are one of the most efficient financial alternatives available. Even if it requires a heavy burden in terms of paperwork, the benefit of the support obtained will far outweigh the bureaucratic inconvenience.

2. The main idea of this text is that:

   A. new US small businesses often fail to plan the small details that are necessary for their success.

   B. new US small businesses lack the money they need to devote to product and technology development.

   C. government grants require a heavy burden in terms of paperwork.

   D. new US small business people sometimes need to turn to friends and family members for financial assistance.

Question 3 refers to the following passage.

Employers use a range of different methods to recruit employees and employees use a range of different methods to look for work. If there is balance in the labor market, employers will be able to find employees easily and people seeking work will be able to find jobs easily. At the same time, wages and earnings should be stable or rise in line with national trends. Where employers cannot fill their vacancies with workers of the desired qualifications, they have skill-shortage vacancies and may respond by raising the earnings offered to potential recruits. In the same way that drivers pay higher prices for fuel when gasoline and diesel supplies are scarce, raising the wages and salaries offered indicates an excess of employer demand over labor supply in the local area.

3. Which of the following can be inferred from the analogy between employers with skill-shortage vacancies and drivers?

   A. Fuel consumption increases during periods of scarcity.

   B. Increased prices cause demand to dwindle.

   C. Scarcity can be defined as an excess of demand over supply.

   D Reports to surveys often exacerbate the problems of shortages.

Question 4 refers to the following passage.

The average consumer does not appreciate that computer monitors contain gases and other toxins that leach into the soil if placed in landfill sites. Simply stated, the gases inside a monitor need to be released safely; without doing so, the ground and air will become filled with these toxic gases. Computers should be disposed of at participating recyclers. A small fee will may be charged for this service, but it is money wisely spend to protect the environment. Nevertheless, it is lamentable that some computer users dispose of their unwanted equipment illegally in order to avoid paying this small fee.

Many people express concern about ways to clean up landfill sites that already have computer monitors dumped in them, but the cost would be in the millions to do such a huge project of this sort. Others argue that the computer equipment that has been in landfills for some time now should be left alone, having already done the harm it could do.

4. What is the main cause of environmental damage from computer monitor disposal today?

    A. Toxic gases from computers that are not disposed of properly are being released into the earth and atmosphere.

    B. There are not enough groups and organizations raising awareness about computer recycling.

C. Some computer users dispose of their unwanted equipment illegally.

D. There is apathy about ways to clean up landfill sites that already have computer equipment dumped in them.

Question 5 refers to the following passage.

Researchers working on the American Life Project found that the popularity of blogs today in terms of readerships in the United States is absolutely exploding. Given that blogs are the best intermediary between websites and forums, it is hard to imagine that there will be a decrease in the popularity of blogs; further, it is not difficult to imagine that they will improve significantly in the future, in keeping with innovations since their inception. In the short term, it is fairly safe to say that larger blogs will use more forms of video technology while older blogs might stick with easy, faster-loading models. One can also surmise that blog indexing methods will continue to improve and may even break away from traditional algorithms.

5. According to the writer, what is the main advantage of blogs?

A. They provide a link between websites and forums.

B. They experiment with video technology.

C. They deploy faster-loading models.

D. They will cause the traditional algorithm method to be superseded.

Question 6 refers to the following passage.

The question of the mechanics of motion is complex and one that has a protracted history. As early as the third century BC, a Greek philosopher and natural scientist named Aristotle conducted scientific investigation into the subject. Most of Aristotle's life was devoted to the study of the objects of natural science, and it is for this work that he is most renowned. The Greek scientist wrote a book entitled *Metaphysics*, which contains the observations that he made as a result of performing this original research in the natural sciences.

In the first century AD, Ptolemy, another Greek scientist, was credited with a nascent, yet unformulated theory, that there was a force that moved toward the center of the earth, thereby holding objects on its surface. Although later ridiculed for his belief that the earth was the center of the planetary system, Aristotle's compatriot nevertheless did contribute to the development of the theory of gravity.

6. According to the passage, what statement best describes Aristotle?

    A. He was the founder of the law of gravity.

    B. He was best-known for producing error-free work.

    C. He was a contemporary of Ptolemy.

    D. He was a famous Greek natural scientist.

Question 7 refers to the following passage.

Cultural and critical theorists have joined in the recent debate about socio-economic status and equality. Focusing on the effect of cultural technologies and systems, they state that various forms of media promote the mechanisms of economic manipulation and oppression. Watching television, they claim, causes those of lower socio-economic class to view themselves as apolitical and powerless victims of the capitalistic machine. Of course, such a viewpoint has a deleterious impact upon individual identity and human motivation.

7. What is the main idea of this passage?

   A. Socio-economic status and equality are extremely complex subjects.

   B. There have been recent debates about socio-economic status and equality.

   C. Certain researchers believe that televisual media can have a negative impact upon socio-economic status and equality.

   D. Watching television is more common in lower class communities.

Question 8 refers to the following passage.

Nowadays adventurers, fieldwork assistants, volunteers, and travelers are replacing tourists. However, the word "tourist" will never completely vanish. There might still be those who quietly travel to foreign lands for nothing other than their own enjoyment, but it will be a clandestine and frowned-upon activity. No one will want to admit to being one of those people.

Bali and Burma have decided to prohibit tourists from entering certain areas of their countries. New territories are being added to the list of places we cannot explore. An international tourist organization lists China, Botswana, Belize, Zanzibar, East Africa, Peru, and Thailand as having areas that have been adversely affected by tourism. They believe that tourists destroy the environment and local cultures. They also assert that although tourists bring money to the local economy, they must be stopped at any price.

8. How does the passage support its claim that tourism will become a clandestine and frowned-upon activity?

    A. by criticizing the types of travelers that have replaced tourists.

    B. by stating that people will still want to travel for their own enjoyment.

    C. by mentioning the economic aspects of tourism.

    D. by citing specific countries that have been negatively impacted by tourism.

Question 9 refers to the following passage.

The nation has seen an increase in publicized knife crimes recently, with many front-page newspaper stories devoted to the latest victim of another vicious attack. Last summer, for instance, a 22-year-old man was stabbed in Central Park in yet another high-profile case. While media attention has increased dramatically in the last few years, the actual figures show that knife crime has remained reasonably constant at around 7 to 8 percent of all crime. However, these figures will do little to appease the victims of the stabbings and knife attacks that have made the news headlines.

9. The writer suggests that members of the public may view knife crime as an exigent social problem primarily because:

    A. a man was stabbed recently in Central Park.

    B. there has been more newspaper publicity devoted to knife crimes recently.

    C. it is difficult to deal with the victims of the attacks.

    D. knife crime has increased dramatically in recent years.

Question 10 refers to the following passage.

Results of a survey on social trends have identified a rise in immigration as the most significant social change in recent years. Population patterns have changed dramatically because immigration has become the main catalyst for population growth. Homegrown population increases, defined as the surplus of births over deaths, have been surpassed by immigration. In other words, immigration has increased, while natural population growth has fallen. This amounts to a huge shift in the importance of immigration to changes in the population, with consequences for ethnic mix and structure. Most people regard immigration as positive phenomenon which has benefited the country. Benefits include skills brought by workers needed to expand the information technology industry. The younger age profile of immigrants would also help to balance the pressures of an aging population.

10. From this passage, one can conclude that:

   A. Young immigrants provide financial support to the elderly.

   B. Immigration will continue to rise in the future.

   C. There is a wider variety of ethnic groups in the country now than previously.

   D. Governmental programs are being over-stretched by recent increases in immigration.

Question 11 refers to the following passage.

Gene splicing, the process whereby a small part of the DNA of one organism is removed and inserted into the DNA chain of another organism, has produced results like the super tomato. In order to create the super tomato, the gene resistant to cold temperatures on the DNA chain of a particular type of cold-water fish was isolated, removed, and inserted into an ordinary tomato plant. This resulted in a new type of tomato plant that can thrive in cold weather conditions.

11. From this passage, it seems safe to conclude that:

   A. the super tomato was the first case of gene splicing.

   B. the super tomato is only one example of gene splicing.

   C. DNA from tomatoes has also been inserted into certain types of fish.

   D. many people object to gene splicing.

Question 12 refers to the following passage.

In 1804, Meriwether Lewis and William Clark began an expedition across the western United States, then known as the Louisiana Territory. The two men had met years earlier and established a long-lasting friendship. When Lewis was later a young captain in the army, he received a letter from President Thomas Jefferson offering him funding to explore the western country. With Jefferson's permission, Lewis offered a partnership in the expedition to his friend Clark. When their journey had safely concluded eight thousand miles later, the two men had made countless discoveries about our nation.

12. The purpose of the passage is:

    A. to give information about Lewis and Clark's westward expedition.

    B. to defend the purchase of the Louisiana Territory.

    C. to state a crucial decision made by Thomas Jefferson.

    D. to compare the skills of Lewis and Clark.

Question 13 refers to the following passage.

The Watergate burglary had many aspects, but at its center was President Richard Nixon. Throughout the investigation of the burglary, government officials denied involvement in the crime. An extensive cover-up operation followed in an attempt to conceal those who were involved in planning the break-in. This subterfuge failed when the FBI investigated the one-hundred dollar bills that were found in the pockets of the burglars. After making inquiries, the FBI discovered that this money originated from the Committee for the Re-election of the President, thereby confirming governmental involvement. In the end, individuals who had entered the highest branches of the American government to serve and protect the people went to prison instead.

13. What is main reason why the cover-up of the Watergate break-in failed?

    A. because the Committee for the Re-election of the President denied involvement

    B. because of the subterfuge of the FBI

    C. because the burglars' money was traced back to a governmental organization

    D. because its ringleaders went to prison

Question 14 refers to the following passage.

Organic farming has become one of the fastest growing trends in agriculture recently. Over the past ten years, sales of organic products in the United States have increased a staggering 20 percent, with retail sales per year of more than 9 billion dollars. American farmers have realized that organic farming is an incredibly cost-effective method because it can potentially be used to control costs, as well as to appeal to higher-priced markets. Apart from these monetary benefits, organic farming also results in positive ecological outcomes for the environment because the use of chemicals and synthetic materials is prohibited.

14. The main idea of the paragraph is that organic farming:

    A. is a very profitable sector of the agricultural industry.

    B. was less popular ten years ago.

    C. prohibits chemical and synthetic materials.

    D. has grown in popularity recently because it is cost-effective and environmentally-friendly.

Question 15 refers to the following passage.

Cancer occurs when cells in the body begin to divide abnormally and form more cells without control or order. There are some factors which are known to increase the risk of cancer. Smoking is the largest single cause of death from cancer in the United States. In addition, poor food choices increase cancer risk. Indeed, research shows that there is a definite link between the consumption of high-fat food and cancer.

15. From this passage, we can infer that:

    A. a low-fat diet can reduce the risk of cancer.

    B. smoking usually causes cells to divide abnormally.

    C. the consumption of high-fat food has increased in recent years.

    D. most cancer sufferers have made poor food choices.

Reading Practice Test 5 – Explanations for the Answers

1. The correct answer is B. This is an example of a question that asks about the author's purpose. The writer's main purpose is to express the objection that the United States prison system is not efficacious. "Efficacious" means capable of producing the desired effect. Re-offending is not the desired or expected result of a stay in prison. The writer states or implies the other reasons as well, but they are specific examples that serve to create a critical tone that supports his main purpose.

2. The correct answer is B. This is an example of a main idea type of question. The main problem that this text addresses is that new US small businesses lack the money they need to devote to product and technology development. The main idea of the text is expressed in the thesis statement, which is the last sentence of paragraph 1: So, businesses that seek to develop products and technology may fail if they don't borrow the money to do so. Answer A is not supported by the text. Answers C and D are specific points, not main ideas.

3. The correct answer is C. The passage tells us that "in the same way that drivers pay higher prices for fuel when gasoline and diesel supplies are scarce, raising the wages and salaries offered indicates an excess of employer demand over labor supply in the local area." Accordingly, scarcity can be defined as an excess of demand over supply.

4. The correct answer is A. The main cause of environmental damage from computer monitor disposal today is that toxic gases from computers that are not disposed of properly are being released into the earth and atmosphere. Paragraph 1 tells us that

"the gases inside a monitor need to be released safely; without doing so, the ground and air will become filled with these toxic gases."

5. The correct answer is A. The main advantage of blogs is that they provide a link between websites and forums. The second sentence states that "blogs are the best intermediary between websites and forums."

6. The correct answer is D. Aristotle was a famous Greek natural scientist. The second sentence of the passage talks about "a Greek philosopher and natural scientist named Aristotle."

7. The correct answer is B. The main idea of this passage is that there have been recent debates about socio-economic status and equality. The first sentence states the main idea; "Cultural and critical theorists have joined in the recent debate about socio-economic status and equality."

8. The correct answer is D. The passage supports its claim that tourism will become a clandestine and frowned-upon activity by citing specific countries that have been negatively impacted by tourism. The author does this is paragraph two of the passage.

9. The correct answer is B. The writer suggests that members of the public may view knife crime as an exigent social problem primarily because there has been more newspaper publicity devoted to knife crimes recently. The passage states: "While media attention has increased dramatically in the last few years, the actual figures show that knife crime has remained reasonably constant at around 7 to 8 percent of all crime."

10. The correct answer is C. From this passage, one can conclude that there is a wider variety of ethnic groups in the country now than previously. The passage explains that immigration has "consequences for ethnic mix and structure."

11. The correct answer is B. The phrase "results like the super tomato" indicates that the super tomato is only one example. The other ideas are not implied by the passage.

12. The correct answer is A. The passage describes how Lewis and Clark met and why they made their famous expedition together. The passage mentions Thomas Jefferson, but this is only a minor point of the passage. The passage does not defend the purchase, nor does it make any comparisons.

13. The correct answer is C. The key sentence is: "After making inquiries, the FBI discovered that this money originated from the Committee for the Re-election of the President, thereby confirming governmental involvement." This sentence signals the reason why the break in failed when it uses the word "thereby." Answers A and D are mentioned in the passage, but they are not the reason for the failure. Answer B is not stated in the passage. Note that the subterfuge was part of the cover-up, not an action by the FBI.

14. The correct answer is D. The passage mentions both cost-effectiveness and benefits to the environment. In other words, answer D gives the main idea, but answers A, B, and C give specific information.

15. The correct answer is A. The passage states: "Indeed, research shows that there is a definite link between the consumption of high-fat food and cancer." So, conversely, we can understand that a low-fat diet will decrease the chances of getting cancer. The other answers are not implied in the passage.

ASVAB Paragraph Comprehension – Practice Test 6

Question 1 refers to the following passage.

The theory of multiple intelligences (MI) is rapidly replacing the intelligence quotient, or IQ. The IQ, long considered the only valid way of measuring intelligence, can be easily criticized because it inheres in many cultural biases. For this reason, there has been a movement away from the IQ test, which is now seen as an indication of a person's academic ability. On the other hand, multiple intelligence measures practical skills such as spatial, visual, and musical ability.

1. The main idea of the passage is that:

    A. there are cultural biases in the IQ test.

    B. the IQ does not take visual or spatial ability into account.

    C. the theory of multiple intelligence is superior to the concept of IQ.

    D. multiple intelligence is a measure of an individual's practical abilities.

Questions 2 to 4 refer to the following passage.

The pyramids at Giza in Egypt are still among the world's largest structures, even today. The monuments were constructed well before the wheel was invented, and it is notable that the Egyptians had only the most primitive, handmade tools to complete the massive project.

Copper saws were used to cut softer stones, as well as the large wooden posts that levered the stone blocks into their final places. Wooden mallets were used to drive flint wedges into rocks in order to split them. An instrument called an adze, which was similar to what we know today as a wood plane, was employed to give wooden objects the correct finish.

The Egyptians also utilized drills that were fashioned from wood and twine. In order to ensure that the stones were level, wooden rods were joined by strips of twine to check that the surfaces of the stone blocks were flat. Finally, the stone blocks were put onto wooden rockers so that they could more easily be placed into their correct positions on the pyramid.

2. The two tools which were used to place the stones into their final positions on the pyramid were made from which substance?

   A. flint

   B. wood

   C. twine

   D. stone

3. What is the writer's main purpose?

   A. to give a step-by-step explanation of the construction of the Giza pyramids

   B. to compare the construction of the Giza pyramids to that of modern day structures

   C. to give an overview of some of the main implements that were used to construct the Giza pyramids

   D. to highlight the importance of the achievement of the construction of the Giza pyramids

4. Which of the following expresses the attitude of the writer?

   A. It is incredible that the Egyptians were able to construct the pyramids using only hand-made tools.

   B. It is a pity that the wheel was not available to the Egyptians during the construction of the pyramids at Giza.

   C. Modern construction projects could learn from the example of the Giza pyramids.

   D. The most difficult aspect of the project was placing the stones in the correct position on the pyramid.

Question 5 refers to the following passage.

Around the world today, more than a billion people still do not have fresh, clean drinking water available on a daily basis. Hundreds of thousands of people in developing countries die needlessly every year because of the consumption of unclean, disease-ridden water. Simply stated, fresh water saves lives. However, what has been understood only recently is that the provision for fresh water around the globe also protects the environment because it means that those who manage water supplies must evaluate in more detail why and how developed countries consume and pollute their available water. Without this evaluation, an ever-increasing number of individuals will continue to die from water-related diseases.

5. We can conclude from the information in this passage that:

   A. water-related disease will decline in the future.

   B. water-related deaths could be avoided.

C. children are the most vulnerable to water-related disease and death.

D. developed countries manage their water supplies better than developing countries.

Question 6 refers to the following passage.

The corpus of research on Antarctica has resulted in an abundance of factual data. For example, we now know that more than ninety nine percent of the land is completely covered by snow and ice, making Antarctica the coldest continent on the planet. This inhospitable climate has brought about the adaptation of a plethora of plants and biological organisms present on the continent. An investigation into the sedimentary geological formations provides testimony to the process of adaptation. Sediments recovered from the bottom of Antarctic lakes, as well as bacteria discovered in ice, have revealed the history of climate change over the past 10,000 years.

6. According to the passage, the plants and organisms in Antarctica:

A. have survived because of the process of adaptation.

B. are the result of sedimentary geological formations.

C. cover more than 99% of the land surface.

D. grow in the bottom of lakes on the continent.

Questions 7 to 10 refer to the following passage.

An efficient electron microscope can magnify an object by more than one million times its original size. This innovation has thereby allowed scientists to study the precise molecules that constitute human life.

The electron microscope functions by emitting a stream of electrons from a gun-type instrument, which is similar to the <u>apparatus</u> used in an old-fashioned television tube. The electrons pass through an advanced electronic field that is accelerated to millions of volts in certain cases. Before traveling through a vacuum in order to remove oxygen molecules, the electrons are focused into a beam by way of magnetic coils.

Invisible to the naked eye, electron beams can nevertheless be projected onto a fluorescent screen. When striking the screen, the electrons glow and can even be recorded on film. Cameras also use film to capture images.

In the transmission electron microscope, which is used to study cells or tissues, the beam passes through a thin slice of the specimen that is being studied. On the other hand, in the scanning electron microscope, which is used for tasks such as examining bullets and fibers, the beam is reflected. This reflection creates a picture of the specimen line by line.

7. What is the last step in the process by which the beam emanating from the electron microscope is formed?

    A. The electrons pass through an electronic field.

    B. The electrons are accelerated to millions of volts.

C. The electrons travel through a vacuum.

D. The electrons pass through magnetic coils.

8. What is the closest synonym to the word <u>apparatus</u> as it is used in the passage?

    A. machine

    B. electricity

    C. device

    D. tube

9. Which of the following assumptions has influenced the writer?

    A. The electron microscope has proven to be an extremely important invention for the scientific community.

    B. The invention of the electron microscope would have been impossible without the prior invention of the television.

    C. The electron microscope cannot function without projection onto a fluorescent screen.

    D. The transmission electron microscope is inferior to the scanning electron microscope.

10. Which statement does NOT support the logical flow of the text?

    A. This innovation has thereby allowed scientists to study the precise molecules that constitute human life.

B. The electrons pass through an advanced electronic field that is accelerated to millions of volts in certain cases.

C. When striking the screen, the electrons glow and can even be recorded on film.

D. Cameras also use film to capture images.

Question 11 refers to the following passage.

Our ability to measure brain activity is owing to the research of two European scientists. It was in 1929 that electrical activity in the human brain was first discovered. Hans Berger, the German psychiatrist who made the discovery, was despondent to find out, however, that many other scientists quickly dismissed his research. The work of Berger was confirmed three years later when Edgar Adrian, a Briton, clearly demonstrated that the brain, like the heart, is profuse in its electrical activity. Because of Adrian's work, we know that the electrical impulses in the brain, called brain waves, are a mixture of four different frequencies.

11. The purpose of the passage is to describe:

    A. two opposing theories.

    B. important research about brain activity.

    C. a personal opinion about the work of two scientists.

    D. the different types of brain wave frequencies.

Question 12 refers to the following passage.

In the Black Hills, four visages protrude from the side of a mountain. The faces are those of four pivotal United States' presidents: George Washington, Thomas Jefferson, Theodore Roosevelt, and Abraham Lincoln. Washington was chosen on the basis of being the first president. Jefferson was instrumental in the writing of the American Declaration of Independence. Lincoln was selected on the basis of the mettle he demonstrated during the American Civil war, and Roosevelt for his development of Square Deal policy, as well as being a proponent of the construction of the Panama Canal.

12. From this passage, these four presidents were chosen because:

   A. of their outstanding courage.

   B. their faces would be esthetically sympathetic to the natural surroundings.

   C. they helped to improve the national economy.

   D. their work was considered crucial to the progress of the nation.

Question 13 refers to the following passage.

The student readiness educational model is based on the view that students are individuals, each operating at different levels of ability. For some students, this might mean that they are operating above the average ability level of their contemporaries, while others may be functioning at a level that is below average. There are also students who are learning at the optimum learning level because they are being challenged and learning new things, but they do not feel overwhelmed or inundated by the new information. According to the student readiness approach, the onus falls on teachers to create classroom learning activities that will challenge the maximum number of students.

13. This passage is primarily about:

   A. the rationale of one particular educational method.

   B. the individuality of various students.

   C. the burdens placed on teachers.

   D. the shortcomings of teachers and students.

Question 14 refers to the following passage.

The most significant characteristic of any population is its age-sex structure, defined as the proportion of people of each gender in each different age group. The age-sex structure determines the potential for reproduction, and therefore population growth. Thus, the age-sex structure has social policy implications. For instance, a population with a high proportion of elderly citizens needs to consider its governmentally-funded pension schemes and health care systems carefully. Conversely, a greater percentage of young children in the population might imply that educational funding and child welfare policies need to be evaluated. Accordingly, as the composition of a population changes over time, the government may need to re-evaluate its funding priorities.

14. Governmental funding decisions should primarily be based on:

   A. the composition of the age and gender of its population.

   B. the number of elderly citizens in its population.

C. the percentage of children in its population.

D. social policy limitations.

Question 15 refers to the following passage.

Owing to the powerful and destructive nature of tornadoes, there are, perhaps not surprisingly, a number of myths and misconceptions surrounding them. For instance, many people mistakenly believe that tornadoes never occur over rivers, lakes, and oceans; yet, waterspouts, tornadoes that form over bodies of water, often move onshore and cause extensive damage to coastal areas. In addition, tornadoes can accompany hurricanes and tropical storms as they move to land. Another common myth about tornadoes is that damage to structures, like houses and office buildings, can be avoided if windows are opened prior to the impact of the storm.

15. What can be inferred about the public's knowledge of tornadoes?

 A. A large number of people know how to avoid tornado damage.

 B. Most people appreciate the risk of death associated with tornadoes.

 C. Some members of the public know how to regulate the pressure inside buildings.

 D. Many people are not fully aware of certain key information about tornadoes.

Reading Practice Test 6 – Explanations for the Answers

1. The correct answer is C. The passage states that MI "is rapidly replacing . . . IQ." It also states that the IQ test "can be easily criticized." Therefore, answer C gives the main idea. Answers A, B, and D are specific points from the passage.

2. The correct answer is B. The two tools which were used to place the stones into their final positions on the pyramid were made from wood. Paragraph 3 mentions wooden rods and wooden rockers.

3. The correct answer is C. The writer's main purpose is to give an overview of some of the main implements that were used to construct the Giza pyramids. The main purpose of the passage is implied in the last sentence of the first paragraph: "it is notable that the Egyptians had only the most primitive, handmade tools to complete the massive project.

4. The correct answer is A. The writer would agree that it is incredible that the Egyptians were able to construct the pyramids using only hand-made tools. The assumption that the outcome was incredible is shown by the contrast between the words "primitive" and "massive" in the last sentence of paragraph 1.

5. The correct answer is B. The passage uses the phrases "people . . . die needlessly" and "fresh water saves lives." Therefore, it is the writer's viewpoint that the deaths could be avoided. The information in answers A, C, and D is not stated in the passage.

6. The correct answer is A. The passage states: "This inhospitable climate has brought about the adaptation . . ."

7. The correct answer is D. The last step in the process for forming the beam is that the electrons pass through magnetic coils. This answer is found in the last sentence of paragraph 2, which states: "Before traveling through a vacuum in order to remove oxygen molecules, the electrons are focused into a beam by way of magnetic coils." Note that the question focuses on the process of forming the beam in particular, not on the movement of electrons in general, so answer C is incorrect.

8. The correct answer is C. The passage compares the microscope to a television tube in the first sentence of paragraph 2. Both of these items are electronic devices. Machines are larger than devices, so answer A is not the best answer.

9. The correct answer is A. The assumption that has influenced the writer is that the electron microscope has proven to be an extremely important invention for the scientific community. This answer is supported by the second sentence of the first paragraph: "This innovation [i.e., the electron microscope] has thereby allowed scientists to study the precise molecules that constitute human life."

10. The correct answer is D. The statement that "cameras also use film to capture images" does not support the logical flow of the text. Nothing else about cameras is mentioned in the passage.

11. The correct answer is B. For this type of question, you need to look carefully at the topic sentence: Our ability to measure brain activity is owing to the research of two European scientists. This sentence states that the passage is going to talk about brain research. We know that the research is important because the passage states: "Because of Adrian's work, we know that . . ."

12. The correct answer is D. The word "pivotal" in the passage means crucial to the progress of something.

13. The correct answer is A. Answer A is the most general answer. We also know that the paragraph is going to talk about the rationale (or reasons for something) because it begins with the phrase "is based on the view." The other answers provide specific information from the passage.

14. The correct answer is A. This idea is contained in the topic sentence: The most significant characteristic of any population is its age-sex structure, defined as the proportion of people of each gender in each different age group. In the remainder of the passage, the author discusses how this idea relates to governmental funding. The other answers are too specific.

15. The correct answer is D. The passage uses the words "myths," "misconceptions," and "mistakenly" to show that most people do not have the correct knowledge about tornadoes.

ASVAB Paragraph Comprehension – Practice Test 7

Questions 1 to 5 refer to the following passage.

Highly concentrated radioactive waste is lethal and can remain so for thousands of years. Accordingly, the disposal of this material remains an issue in most energy-producing countries around the world. In the United States, for example, liquid forms of radioactive waste are usually stored in stainless steel tanks. For extra protection, the tanks are double-walled and surrounded by a concrete covering that is one meter thick. This storage solution is also utilized the United Kingdom, in most cases.

The long-term problem lies in the fact that nuclear waste generates heat as radioactive atoms decay. This excess heat could ultimately result in a radioactive leak. Therefore, the liquid needs to be cooled by pumping cold water into coils inside the tanks. However, this strategy is only a temporary solution. The answer to the long-term storage of nuclear waste may be fusing the waste into glass cylinders that are stored deep underground.

1. How are the tanks which are used for storing radioactive waste protected against leaks?

    A. They are encased in concrete.

    B. They only contain waste in liquid form.

    C. They are fused into glass cylinders.

    D. They are combined with cold water.

2. Which of the following is the best title for the passage?

    A. Radioactive Waste in the US and UK

B. Current Storage Solutions for Radioactive Waste, Potential Problems, and Long-Term Solutions

C. Radioactive Waste: The Long-Term Risks

D. The Threat of Radioactive Waste and the Creation of Glass Cylinders

3. Which of the following assumptions has most influenced the writer?

A. The threat of a radioactive leak is exaggerated by the public.

B. The storage of radioactive waste in stainless steel tanks is extremely dangerous.

C. The United Kingdom normally follows practices that the United States has adopted.

D. A radioactive leak would have disastrous consequences around the globe.

4. In the second paragraph of the passage, "this strategy" refers to which of the following?

A. the danger of the consequences of the escape of radioactive substances from the storage tanks

B. the generation of nuclear waste as radioactive atoms decay

C. the process of cooling the liquid by means of cold water

D. the fact that the solution is only viable on a short-term basis

5. The author's attitude can best be described as one of:

A. apprehension

B. disillusionment

C. shock

D. contempt

Question 6 refers to the following passage.

Earthquakes occur when there is motion in the tectonic plates on the surface of the earth. The crust of the earth contains twelve such tectonic plates, which are from four to ten kilometers in length when located below the sea, although those on land can be from thirty to seventy kilometers long. Fault lines, the places where these plates meet, build up a great deal of pressure because the plates are constantly pressing on each other. Thus, the two plates will eventually shift or separate because the pressure on them is constantly increasing, and this build-up of energy needs to be released. When the plates shift or separate, we have the occurrence of an earthquake, also known as a seismic event. The point where the earthquake is at its strongest is called the epicenter. Waves of motion travel out from this epicenter, often causing widespread destruction to an area.

6. What happens immediately after the pressure on the tectonic plates has become too great?

    A. Fault lines are created.

    B. There is a build-up of energy.

    C. There is a seismic event.

    D. Waves of motion travel out from the epicenter.

Question 7 refers to the following passage.

The Hong Kong and Shanghai Bank Corporation (HSBC) skyscraper in Hong Kong is one of the world's most famous high-rise buildings. The building was designed so that it had many pre-built parts that were not constructed on site. This prefabrication made the project a truly international effort: the windows were manufactured in Austria, the exterior walls were fabricated in the United States, the toilets and air-conditioning were made in Japan, and many of the other components came from Germany.

7. The main idea of this passage is that:

   A. prefabricated buildings are more international than those built on site.

   B. countries should work together more often in construction projects.

   C. the HSBC building was an international project.

   D. the HSBC building is well-known because many countries were involved in its construction.

Question 8 refers to the following passage.

In December 406 A.D. in what is now called Germany, fifteen thousand warriors crossed the frozen Rhine River and traveled into the Roman Empire of Gaul. A new historical epoch would soon be established in this former Roman Empire. Even though this period has diminished in historical significance in comparison to more recent events,

the demise of the Roman Empire was certainly unprecedented in the fifth century. The six subsequent centuries that followed the collapse of the Roman Empire formed what we now call the Middle Ages.

8. According to the passage, the Roman Empire of Gaul:

   A. was established during the middle ages.

   B. is now referred to as Germany.

   C. gradually collapsed throughout the Middle Ages.

   D. fell into ruin from 406 to 499 AD.

Question 9 refers to the following passage.

The study of philosophy usually deals with two key problem areas: human choice and human thought. A consideration of both of these problem areas includes scientific and artistic viewpoints on the nature of human life. The first problem area, human choice, asks whether human beings can really make decisions that can change their futures. It also investigates to what extent the individual's future is fixed and pre-determined by cosmic forces outside the control of human beings. In the second problem area, human thought, epistemology is considered. Epistemology means the study of knowledge; it should not be confused with ontology, the study of being or existence.

9. The author's primary purpose is:

    A. to compare two areas of an academic discipline.

    B. to explain key aspects of a particular area of study.

    C. to contrast scientific and artistic views on a particular topic.

    D. to investigate two troublesome aspects of human behavior.

Questions 10 to 12 refer to the following passage.

The world's first public railway carried passengers, even though it was primarily designed to transport coal from inland mines to ports on the North Sea. Unveiled on September 27, 1825, the train had thirty-two open wagons and carried over three hundred people. The locomotive steam engine was powered by what was termed the steam-blast technique. The chimney of the locomotive redirected exhaust steam into the engine via a narrow pipe. In this way, the steam created a draft of air which followed after it, creating more power and speed for the engine.

The train had rimmed wheels which ran atop rails that were specially designed to give the carriages a faster and smoother ride. While the small carriages could hardly be termed commodious, the locomotive could accelerate to fifteen miles per hour, a record-breaking speed at that time. Subsequently, the inventor of the locomotive, George Stephenson, revolutionized his steam engine by adding twenty-four further pipes. Now containing twenty-five tubes instead of one, Stephenson's second "iron horse" was even faster and more powerful than his first creation.

10. The word "commodious" means:

   A. small

   B. uncomfortable

   C. spacious

   D. speedy

11. Why was the second locomotive that Stephenson invented an improvement on his first?

   A. because it ran with greater force and speed

   B. because it was more comfortable

   C. because it could carry more passengers

   D. because it contained more pipes and tubes

12. From the information contained in the passage, it seems reasonable to infer which of the following?

   A. Many passengers were frightened about traveling on Stephenson's new locomotive.

   B. George Stephenson's inventions laid the basic foundations for modern day public trains and railways.

   C. Profits in the coal industry increased after the invention of the locomotive.

   D. Stephenson should have been able to invent a locomotive that could run faster.

Question 13 refers to the following passage.

In 1859, some of Abraham Lincoln's associates began to put forward the idea that he should run for president of the United States, a notion that he discounted in his usual self-deprecating manner. However, as time passed, Lincoln began to write influential Republican Party leaders for their support. By 1860, Lincoln had garnered more public support, after having delivered public lectures and political speeches in various states. Despite being the underdog, Lincoln won 354 of the 466 total nominations at the Republican National Convention, and later, in November, 1860, the populace elected Lincoln as President of the United States.

13. This passage is mainly about:

    A. the personal characteristics of Abraham Lincoln.

    B. the results of the 1860 United States election.

    C. how Lincoln ran for and won the United States presidency.

    D. how to be successful as a politician.

Question 14 refers to the following passage.

American Major League Baseball consisted of only a handful of teams when the National League was founded in 1876, but baseball has grown in popularity by leaps and bounds over the years, resulting in increased ticket sales for games and bolstering the profits of its investors. The increased demand from the public, in turn, precipitated the formation of a new division, known as the American League, in 1901. Additionally, new teams are formed from time to time in accordance with regional demand, such as the Colorado Rockies in Denver, Colorado, and the Devil Rays in Tampa Bay, Florida.

14. The main purpose of the passage is:

    A   to give examples of two popular American baseball teams.

    B   to provide specific information about the process of forming new baseball teams.

    C   to trace historical developments relating to the popularity of baseball.

    D   to criticize Americans who depend on baseball for entertainment.

Question 15 refers to the following passage.

Music as we know it around the world today originated in the genre of chanting. Chant, a monophonic form of music, was the dominant mode of music prior to the thirteenth century. The semantic origins of the word "monophonic" are of special interest. "Mono" is from a Greek word which means one thing alone or by itself. "Phonic" is also Greek in origin, and it means sound. Accordingly, monophonic music consists of only one sound or voice that combines various notes in a series.

15. What is the main idea of this passage?

    A. The origins of music in the western world.

    B. The history of music during two previous centuries.

    C. The semantics of a particular Greek word.

    D. The variety of symphonic forms.

Reading Practice Test 7 – Explanations for the Answers

1. The correct answer is A. The tanks are protected against leaks because they are encased in concrete. The fourth sentence of paragraph one states: "For extra protection, the tanks are double-walled and surrounded by a concrete covering that is one meter thick."

2. The correct answer is B. The first two sentences of paragraph one introduce the idea of radioactive waste generally, before moving on to talk about how the waste is stored at the present time. Paragraph two begins by discussing the problems with storing the waste in this way and ends by giving an overview of possible solutions to these problems. So, the best title is "Current Storage Solutions for Radioactive Waste, Potential Problems, and Long-Term Solutions."

3. The correct answer is D. The author implies that a radioactive leak would have dire consequences since he opens the passage with this sentence: "Highly concentrated radioactive waste is lethal and can remain so for thousands of years."

4. The correct answer is C. "This strategy" in the second paragraph of the passage refers to the process of cooling the liquid by means of cold water. For questions like this one, you need to look carefully at the sentence preceding the phrase. The sentence before the words "this strategy" states that "the liquid needs to be cooled by pumping cold water into coils inside the tanks." So, we know that we are talking about the process of cooling the liquid at this point in the passage.

5. The correct answer is A. The author's attitude can best be described as one of apprehension. "Apprehension" means to be worried about something or to sense that

a negative consequence may occur because of something. The author's concern is evident in the first sentence of the passage, which states: "Highly concentrated radioactive waste is lethal and can remain so for thousands of years."

6. The correct answer is C. For questions asking you about the order of steps or events, you need to focus on the part of the selection where the particular step is mentioned. Here, we can see that the question is asking about the occurrence of pressure on the tectonic plates. So, we need to focus on these two sentences from the paragraph: "The two plates will eventually shift or separate because the pressure on them is constantly increasing, and this build-up of energy needs to be released. When the plates shift or separate, we have an occurrence of an earthquake, also known as a seismic event." You also need to pay attention to the words in the question that indicate the sequencing, such as "before," "after," "next," or "during." The question asks us: "What happens immediately *after* the pressure on the tectonic plates has become too great?" The word "after" shows that we need to determine the next step. The selection indicates that after the pressure builds up, it needs to be released. The passage states that the release of energy in this way causes an earthquake, which is also called "a seismic event." So, answer C is correct.

7. The correct answer is C. The passage states: "This prefabrication made the project a truly international effort." Ideas from answers A and B are not mentioned in the passage. The passage does not give the precise reason why the building is famous. It just states that the building is famous.

8. The correct answer is D. The passage states: "the demise of the Roman Empire was certainly unprecedented in the fifth century." We know that "demise" means ruin.

We also know that the invasion took place in 406 AD, and that the fifth century ended in 499 AD.

9. The correct answer is B. The topic sentence states the author's purpose: "The study of philosophy usually deals with two key problem areas." The passage does not make any comparisons or contrasts, nor does it describe human behavior as "troublesome." It merely describes the key areas as "problem areas."

10. The correct answer is C. The word "commodious" means spacious. This is in contrast to the word "small" at the beginning of the sentence.

11. The correct answer is A. The second locomotive that Stephenson invented was an improvement on his first because it ran with greater force and speed. The last sentence of the passage states that "Stephenson's second 'iron horse' was even faster and more powerful than his first creation."

12. The correct answer is B. From the information contained in the passage, it seems reasonable to infer that George Stephenson's inventions laid the basic foundations for modern day public trains and railways. The passage describes how George Stephenson invented the steam locomotive and the world's first public railway. Such inventions lay the basic foundations, which can later be improved upon with advances in technology.

13. The correct answer is C. The main idea of the passage is to give information about how Lincoln became the president. Answers A and B are too specific, and answer D is an overgeneralization.

14. The correct answer is C. We know that the passage is going to give historical information because the topic sentence [defined as the first sentence of a paragraph] contains the phrase "was founded in 1876." Answers A and B give specific points that are mentioned in the passage, not the main idea. Answer D is incorrect because no criticisms are stated in the passage.

15. The correct answer is A. The topic sentence contains the word "originated." Only one century is mentioned in the passage, so answer B is incorrect. Answer C is too specific. Answer D is not stated in the passage.

ASVAB Paragraph Comprehension – Practice Test 8

Question 1 refers to the following passage.

The use of computers in the stock market helps to control national and international finance. These controls were originally designed in order to create long-term monetary stability and protect shareholders from catastrophic losses. Nevertheless, the high level of automation now involved in buying and selling shares means that computer-to-computer trading could result in a downturn in the stock market. Such a slump in the market, if not properly regulated, could bring about a computer-led stock market crash. For this reason, regulations have been put in place by NASDAQ, AMEX, and FTSE.

1. From this passage, one could infer that:

    A. Regulations on computer-to-computer trading are considered to be a financial necessity.

    B. There are negative public views about regulations on computer-to-computer trading.

    C. NASDAQ, AMEX, and FTSE were initially opposed to establishing regulations on computer-to-computer trading.

    D. The role of computers in international markets has not been modified over time.

Question 2 refers to the following passage.

Airline travel is generally considered to be an extremely safe mode of transportation. Statistics reveal that far fewer individuals are killed each year in airline accidents than in crashes involving automobiles. In spite of this safety record, airlines are subject to ever-increasingly strict standards when investigating aircraft crashes. Information gleaned from the investigation of aircraft crashes is utilized in order to prevent such tragedies from occurring again in the future.

2. The main purpose of this passage is:

   A. to contrast automotive travel with airline travel.

   B. to compare statistics on deaths related to transportation accidents.

   C. to explain the reasons for the investigation of aircraft crashes.

   D. to justify government spending on aircraft accident investigations.

Questions 3 to 7 refer to the following information.

How is civil order maintained within any given population? The civil order control function suggests that public order is best maintained through agencies other than the police force or militia. Accordingly, martial law, the establishment of military rule over a civilian population, is only imposed when other methods of civil control have proven ineffective. Either the leader of a country's military system or of the country's own government may lay down the edict for the rule of martial law. In the past, this state of affairs most commonly occurred to quell uprisings during periods of colonial occupation or to thwart a coup, defined as an illegal and usually violent seizure of a government by a select group of individuals.

So, how is the declaration of martial law currently regulated? The constitutions of many countries now make provisions for the introduction of martial law, allowing it only in cases of national emergency or in the case of threats to national security from foreign countries. In democratic nations, severe restrictions are imposed on the implementation of martial law, meaning that a formal declaration of military rule over a nation should be rendered virtually impractical. In spite of these democratic systems being in place, forms of military control are still instituted during times of crisis, with a country's military system being mobilized to support civil authorities, such as municipalities and local police forces. The United States Secretary of State recently commented: "The use of military force to control the population is still a necessary albeit inimical outcome for the governments of certain countries around the globe today."

3. Which of the following statements best explains the differences between how martial law was instituted in the past and how it is instituted at present?

   A. In the past, the militia was not used to support civil authorities, although it is used this way at present.

   B. In the past, countries did not have constitutions or other established means to regulate the declaration of martial law.

   C. There are more threats to national security nowadays than there were in the past.

   D. Civil order was more difficult to maintain in the past than it is during the present time.

4. It can be inferred from the passage that the United States Secretary of State would agree with which of the following statements?

   A. The declaration of martial law is sometimes needed, although it is usually undesirable.

   B. The declaration of martial law is a pragmatic remedial solution when a population is out of control.

   C. The country's military system should provide more support for civil authorities.

   D. The police forces of most municipalities are already over-burdened with other tasks.

5. The last sentence of the first paragraph suggests that which of the following is true of coups?

   A. They usually represent a large proportion of the population.

   B. They no longer occur as countries now have controls in place to prevent them.

   C. They may involve assassinating or harming government leaders, officials, or citizens.

   D. They have taken place most frequently during periods of colonial occupation.

6. The author finds fault with the civil order control function for its failure to address which of the following?

   A. the maintenance of civil order in democratic nations

   B. the regulation of the declaration of martial law at present

   C. the reasons why uprisings took place in colonial times

   D. the reasons why democratic nations still sometimes deploy the military to impose order on their populations

7. It can be inferred that the author of the passage would agree with the basic tenet of the civil order control function for which of the following reasons?

   A. Police forces are well trained and can readily respond during times of crisis.

   B. Public order and civil control are not as important as other social issues.

   C. A country's military can best control the civilian population.

   D. There are occasions when public order can only be reinstated through the establishment of military rule, in spite of the disadvantages in doing so.

Question 8 refers to the following passage.

In 1749, British surveyors spotted a high peak in the distant range of the Himalayas. More than one hundred years later, in 1852, another survey was completed, which confirmed that this peak was the highest mountain in the world. Later named Mount Everest, this peak was considered to be the world's highest mountain until 1986. At that time, George Wallerstein from the University of Washington posited that another Himalayan mountain, named K-2, was higher than Everest. It took an expedition of Italian scientists, who used a surfeit of technological devices, to disprove Wallerstein's claim.

8. According to the passage, which one of the following statements is correct?

    A. Since 1749, Mount Everest has universally been considered to be the tallest mountain in the world.

    B. Wallerstein fell into disrepute in the academic community after his claims were disproved.

    C. The Italian team confirmed that Everest was, in fact, the tallest mountain in the world.

    D. In spite of a lack of technologically-advanced equipment, Italian scientists were able to refute Wallerstein's hypothesis.

Question 9 refers to the following passage.

Clones have been used for centuries in the field of horticulture. For instance, florists have traditionally made clones of geraniums and other plants by taking cuttings and re-planting them in fresh soil. Despite the predictability of cloning in the realm of plants and flowers, cloning has arguably taken on sinister undertones, thanks to the rapid development of science and technology. Some fear the ethical ramifications that will inevitably occur if cloning is extended to the human species.

9. We can conclude from the information in this passage that:

    A. cloning is a somewhat controversial subject.

    B. cloning has fallen out of favor with horticulturalists.

    C. in spite of certain misgivings, many people support human cloning.

    D. technological advances have impeded the use of cloning.

Questions 10 to 12 refer to the following passage.

The Earth's only natural satellite, the Moon lacks its own atmosphere and is only about one-fourth the size of the planet it orbits. The equality of its orbital rate to that of the Earth is the result of gravitational locking, also known as synchronous rotation. Thus, the same hemisphere of the Moon always faces the earth. The brightest lunar surface areas are formed from meteoric material, while its dark surface regions consist of mare basalts.

Lunar evolution models suggest that the development of the Moon occurred in five principle stages: (1) increase in mass followed by large-scale melting; (2) separation of the crust with concurrent bombardment by meteors; (3) melting at greater depth; (4) lessening of meteoric bombardment with further melting at depth and the formation of basaltic plains; and (5) the cessation of volcanic activity followed by gradual internal cooling. Because of the geological and mineral composition of the surface of the Moon, one popular theory hypothesizes that the Moon grew out of debris that was dislodged from the Earth's crust following the impact of a large object with the planet.

10. For which of the following situations does the concept of synchronous rotation, as it is defined in the passage, provide the most likely explanation?

    A. The Moon goes through four phases every twenty-eight days.

    B. A star appears to shine at the same intensity, regardless of its position in the sky.

    C. Two objects fall to the ground at the same speed and land at the same time.

    D. A telecommunications satellite is always in the same position above a certain city on Earth.

11. The passage suggests that which one of the following probably occurred after the completion of the process of lunar evolution?

    A. Ice continued to melt on the surface of the Moon.

    B. The temperature of the internal core of the Moon was lower than it was previously.

C. The likelihood of the collision of the Moon with a meteor was substantially reduced.

D. There were further eruptions of magma or lava.

12. Which of the following, if true, would tend to disprove the hypothesis that the Moon grew out of debris that was dislodged from the Earth's crust?

    A. An analysis reveals that there are no geological similarities between samples of material from the surface of the Moon and material from the Earth's crust.

    B. The Moon has been found not to have had any previous volcanic activity.

    C. Many meteors bombarded with the Earth during the process of lunar evolution.

    D. A great deal of debris is created when a meteor collides with the Earth.

Question 13 refers to the following passage.

Educational psychology studies pupils in a classroom setting in order to help educators to understand the behaviors and attitudes that affect learning and teaching. This branch of psychology was a reaction against the psychometric movement, which tested students in order to place them into "streamed" classes of different ability levels. The popularity of IQ testing and streamed education declined in the second half of the twentieth century, and the education profession is now focused on developing programs that view students as individuals and advising schools how better to function as organizations.

13. According to the passage, the best way to distinguish between the education profession before the second half of the twentieth century and current educational practice would be by:

   A. looking at the results of psychometric testing.

   B. studying pupils in a classroom setting.

   C. supporting the benefits of IQ testing.

   D. determining whether students are grouped into categories based on test results.

Question 14 refers to the following passage.

Jean Piaget was one of the most influential thinkers in the area of child development in the twentieth century. Piaget posited that children go through a stage of assimilation as they grow to maturity. Assimilation refers to the process of transforming one's environment in order to bring about its conformance to innate cognitive schemes and structures. Schemes used in infant breast feeding and bottle feeding are examples of assimilation because the child utilizes his or her innate capacity for sucking to complete both tasks.

14. Why does the writer mention bottle feeding in the above paragraph?

   A. to identify one of the important features of assimilation

   B. to exemplify the assimilation process

   C. to describe the importance of assimilation

   D. to explain difficulties children face during assimilation

Question 15 refers to the following passage.

Inherent social and cultural biases pervaded the manner in which archeological findings were investigated during the early nineteenth century because little attention was paid to the roles that wealth, status, and nationality played in the recovery and interpretation of artifacts. However, in the 1860s Charles Darwin established the theory that human beings are the ultimate product of a long biological evolutionary process. Darwinian theory infiltrated the discipline of archeology and heavily influenced the manner in which archeological artifacts were recovered and analyzed. As a result of Darwinism, there was a surge in artifacts excavated from African and Asian localities by the late 1900s.

15. Based on the information above, what can be inferred about the early 1900s?

    A. There were few archeological findings from Africa and Asia.

    B. Darwinian theory had little effect on archeology.

    C. All archeological findings were culturally biased in the early 1900s.

    D. Charles Darwin was responsible for the recovery of many artifacts.

Reading Practice Test 8 – Explanations for the Answers

1. The correct answer is A. The passage states that "computer-to-computer trading could result in a downturn in the stock market." Further, this downturn could result in a "computer-led stock market crash." In order to avoid these negative results, the regulations are needed. Answers B and C are not stated in the passage. Answer D is incorrect because the passage talks about how the use of computers has changed over time.

2. The correct answer is C. The last sentence of the passage explains the purpose of or reasons for the aircraft crash investigations. Answers A and B are too specific. Answer D is not stated in the passage.

3. The correct answer is B. In the past, countries did not have constitutions or other established means to regulate the declaration of martial law. The second paragraph explains that "the constitutions of many countries now make provisions for the introduction of martial law." The use of the word "now" suggests that these provisions were not in place in the past.

4. The correct answer is A. It can be inferred from the passage that the United States Secretary of State would agree with the statement that the declaration of martial law is sometimes needed, although it usually undesirable. We know this because the last sentence of the passage states that, according to the United States Secretary of State, martial law is a "necessary albeit inimical outcome." "Inimical" means undesirable or unfavorable.

5. The correct answer is C. The last sentence of the first paragraph states that a coup is "defined as an illegal and usually violent seizure of a government by a select group of individuals." The use of the word "violent" suggests that other people may be killed or harmed.

6. The correct answer is D. The author finds fault with the civil order control function for its failure to address the reasons why democratic nations still sometimes deploy the military to impose order on their populations. In paragraph 1, the writer explains that "the civil order control function suggests that public order is best maintained through agencies other than the police force or militia." However, the writer explains in paragraph 2 that "in spite of these democratic systems being in place, forms of military control are still instituted during times of crisis, with a country's military system being mobilized to support civil authorities, such as municipalities and local police forces."

7. The correct answer is D. It can be inferred that the author of the passage would agree with the basic tenet of the civil order control function because there are occasions when public order can only be reinstated through the establishment of military rule, in spite of the disadvantages in doing so. In paragraph 1, the author writes that "martial law, the establishment of military rule over a civilian population, is only imposed when other methods of civil control have proven ineffective." So, the author believes that martial law should only be used when the civil order control function, which is usually the best option, has failed.

8. The correct answer is C. The last sentence of the passage states: "It took an expedition of Italian scientists, who used a surfeit of technological devices, to

disprove Wallerstein's claim." In other words, the Italians proved that Everest was in fact higher than K-2. Note that the word "surfeit" means a large or abundant amount of something.

9. The correct answer is A. The words "sinister undertones" and "arguably" in the passage demonstrate that cloning is a controversial subject. Answer C is not implied in the passage. There is information in the passage to suggest that answers B and D are incorrect.

10. The correct answer is D. The concept of synchronous rotation, as it is defined in the passage, provides the most likely explanation for the situation in which a telecommunications satellite is always in the same position above a certain city on Earth. This is similar to the way in which the same hemisphere of the Moon always faces the earth.

11. The correct answer is B. Point 5 in paragraph 2 states that the last step in lunar evolution was "the cessation of volcanic activity followed by gradual internal cooling." So, we can conclude that after lunar evolution, the temperature of the internal core of the Moon was lower than it was previously.

12. The correct answer is A. An analysis revealing that there are no geological similarities between samples of material from the surface of the Moon and material from the Earth's crust would tend to disprove the hypothesis that the Moon grew out of debris that was dislodged from the Earth's crust. If we assume that the Moon grew out of material from the Earth, we would expect to see some geological similarities.

13. The correct answer is D. According to the passage, the best way to distinguish between the education profession before the second half of the twentieth century and current educational practice is by determining whether students are grouped into categories based on test results. The passage explains that students used to be placed "into 'streamed' classes of different ability levels." However, current education practice is to "view students as individuals."

14. The correct answer is B. When explaining the idea of assimilation, the passage uses the phrase "are examples of" to show that breast and bottle feeding are being used as examples. Note that the word "exemplify" means to give an example.

15. The correct answer is A. The passage concludes by stating: "there was a surge in artifacts excavated from African and Asian localities by the late 1900s." "Surge" means to increase suddenly from a small or low amount. If these findings suddenly increased at the end of the century, one could assume that they were limited at the beginning of the century. Answers B and D are incorrect according to the passage. Answer C is an overgeneralization.

NOTES:

www.ingramcontent.com/pod-product-compliance
Lightning Source LLC
Chambersburg PA
CBHW081351080526
44588CB00016B/2448